I Will
Remember
You

I Will Remember You

What to do when someone you love dies

A guidebook through grief for teens

by Laura Dower

Introduction and commentary
by Elena Lister, M.D.

SCHOLASTIC INC.
New York   Toronto   London   Auckland   Sydney
Mexico City   New Delhi   Hong Kong

No part of this publication may be reproduced in whole or in part, or stored in a retrieval system, or transmitted in any form or by any means, electronic, mechanical, photocopying, recording, or otherwise, without written permission of the publisher. For information regarding permission, write to Scholastic Inc., Attention: Permissions Department, 555 Broadway, New York, NY 10012.

ISBN 0-439-13961-9

Copyright © 2001 by Laura Dower.

All rights reserved. Published by Scholastic Inc. SCHOLASTIC and associated logos are trademarks and/or registered trademarks of Scholastic Inc.

Cover design by Steve Scott.

12 11 10 9 8 7 6 5 4 3 2 1   1 2 3 4 5 6/0

Printed in the U.S.A.

First Scholastic printing, April 2001

For Liza

*Dedicated to teens everywhere
who grieve . . . and remember.*

Table of Contents

VI. Helping 175

Chapter 15: When Someone Else Is Grieving . 177

Chapter 16: Finding Professional Help 186

Conclusion 195

Appendix: Other Bereavement Resources . . 197

Acknowledgments

Thank you to the many gone but not forgotten who have helped me to personally shape the development of this book, especially Joseph "Papa" Hurley, Kip Haris, Ronnie Rosenberg, Katherine Dower, and Ary Corneille.

Thanks to my editor, Jean Feiwel, for giving me this project and entrusting me with her (and my) vision of it; and to her assistant Robin Wasserman, for her energy, intelligence, and unflappable spirit. You helped me get it right. Thanks also to Steve Scott and his team of designers for making the pages come to life.

To Elena Lister, whose wisdom about teens and grief guided the book through all of its stages. I wish I could place a cow on every one of the pages. Thanks, also, to Marjorie Kaplan, M.D., for her suggestions.

To Gifford Booth, TAI, and Julia Cameron's *The Artist's Way*, thanks for unending inspiration.

To my husband Rich, for giving me the support, love, energy, and compassion I needed while writing about such a hard subject.

Finally, of course, to teens everywhere who contributed to this book with a private thought or poem, thank you for your honesty and intensity. Your words inspire me to feel, think, and live, even through grief. You have shared something invaluable that I hope other teens will be able to find and express for themselves.

— Laura Dower

I would never have survived Liza's death — nonetheless been able to participate in this book — without Phil and Molly. Phil gives me such steadfast love, wisdom, and humor. He has monumental capacity to endure feelings and huge reservoirs of strength. Molly's "magic" buoys me daily and shows me how much there is still to live for.

Many friends and family members — and they know who they are — taught me what being there for someone *really* means. It is those I was able to accompany as they unflinchingly faced their own deaths — Liza, Sumner, and Shira — who taught me how not to be afraid.

Last but not least, I want to say how much I learned from Laura Dower. She was generous enough to let me accompany her on this book venture. Our collaboration was a joy for me because of her intelligence, sense of humor, creativity, and remarkable openness.

— Elena Lister, M.D.

Author Note

Please note that all counseling-related information in this book has been reviewed with Elena Lister, M.D., psychiatrist, analyst, and adolescent and teen grief counselor. Her many years of professional and personal experience have shaped the evolution of the text. However, also remember that the material here represents the feelings and opinions of only two individuals. There is always a chance that self-help suggestions like these may not be enough to help you through your grief. Do not feel discouraged. Sometimes you will need the help of an *objective* third party, whether that person is a licensed therapist, rabbi, priest, or other counselor, to get you through your grieving experience. Do not hesitate to seek additional help when you're dealing with the subjects of this book.

— Laura Dower
April, 2001

Introduction

"I will remember you."

This is what I promised my almost-six-year-old daughter, Liza, the week before she died. I said it to her in hundreds of ways — in hugs and snuggles and by telling her "You will always be in my heart" and "A part of you will stay alive in me, and a part of me will die with you." However I put it, what started out as a promise to her has become one of my most sustaining comforts, now that she is gone.

This is not my prescription on how to handle dying or death. Rather, it is my way to explain to you how I came to know — really know — what we are capable of bearing if we are not emotionally alone. Even unspeakable loss is speakable; indeed has to be, I believe, in order for us to live on.

Liza was diagnosed with leukemia just days after her fourth birthday. My husband, our then-seven-year-old daughter, Molly, Liza, and I were all catapulted into the world of the sick. My husband or I spent the next twenty-one months in the hospital with Liza (she coined the term "houscpital" to express that) rather than at home as her illness and its treatments became more and more debilitating. Although every day I thought about and feared her dying, and although many days we faced life-threatening symptoms, we were fighting the fight and going for a cure. Because it was still possible.

And then Liza relapsed once more, one last time, and her doctors told us she would die — anytime from a week to a year from that surreal-seeming day. Then we lived together, every minute facing her certain and imminent death. Liza sensed she was dying even before she pointedly asked me to confirm it later that same night. "Mommy, I know that I am going to die from my leukemia," she began. Then, in sequence, narrowing her window of remaining life to a smaller and smaller future, she said, "Will I get to be a mommy? Will I get to be a teenager? Will I make it to be seven?" Liza knew how she wanted to die and proceeded to tell me. "I want to die on your lap, Mommy. I want you to die with me. No! No! I want you to die right after me so you can be with me when I die."

I was determined, as I had been throughout her illness, to not leave Liza emotionally alone with anything she had to face. Liza lived three more months, propelled through pain and deterioration by her powerful wish to learn to read and make it to her sixth birthday before she died. And she did indeed die in the arms of the three of us, at home. Some of her last words were to Molly, then nine. "It's my time to die, and I want you to know that I love you," she said.

During Liza's last months, many people commented to us about how hard it must be to manage all of the medicines and IVs and machines. I said then, as I do now . . . that was the easy part.

Learning to live *without* her was, is, and always will be the hard part. That is how I came to be a part of this book.

I do remember her, but the kind of real, inside-the-heart remembering that sustains me took time. At first I searched ceaselessly for external confirmations that she had existed, had mattered to others, had left her imprint on the world. Realization (with the name "Liza" held within it) became one of my favorite words. Then, slowly, outside connections to her became less urgent, and I could feel the enduring power of all that she had taught me, all that I had learned about myself and the people I love as we traversed this most awful part of my life.

I realized that the worst time was also, in its intensity and intimacy, the most meaningful time. I learned that I could go forward with my life and simultaneously embrace who she was. In tribute to Liza, I want to help others find their way as they face loss. I now devote much of my lifework to dealing with death and dying. I work with individuals, in school communities, and with medical professionals, helping people talk about death.

Many people could not talk with us about Liza or her death after she died. When any mention of her name would have been music to my ears, such people ignored the topic or avoided us. As a society, we are so frightened by death that we leave those who are grieving alone with it. Then it feels all the more unbearable and unresolvable.

But grief is about living.

Grief is about finding a way not to move on past but to move along with who this person was to you. Each person must do this in his or her own way. This book is one way to feel less alone as you do so. The teen years are often filled with feelings of being alone as you face powerful emotions. I want to help you ease that burden and embrace your struggle, as you consider and reconsider who you are and what your world is about. You can know and talk about all the powerful feelings you encounter when facing loss.

— Elena Lister, M.D.
New York, NY

Preface

I will remember you.
Will you remember me?

— from "I Will Remember You"
by Sarah McLachlan

This is a book about grieving. . . .
About how to go on living when someone dies.
About how to say good-bye to someone you love.
And maybe even how to say hello . . . to yourself.
Dealing with death is tough stuff. This book may bring up painful feelings and help you to feel. Many times a major loss reveals what's hidden beneath your surface, and you may not like what you see. Try not to panic.
Teen grief can be especially challenging. Right now you may be spending so much time trying new things, befriending new people, and taking in new information at school, home, and elsewhere that you may not have taken a recent inventory of your feelings. Now, after a death has happened, emotions you haven't even said hello to in years (or *ever*) are making guest appearances in your day-to-day life.
That can be a little disarming.
But there is a light at the end of this long, winding tunnel.
By exploring your grieving process, you'll trace unique patterns of your own responses and emotions. You'll be able to see exactly where you tune in, tune out, and tune back in again. You'll see that powerful feelings are not to be feared. You'll see *yourself*.
Whatever you do, don't give up.
Keep reading, even if it hurts. That hurt is like an alarm going off inside of you, begging you to listen to yourself.

Grief is *not* an illness but a natural response to loss. Your "alarm" is a natural response. Try to hear it.

Wouldn't it be nice if this were a book on steps A to Z of grief? Start here, and two weeks later you'll end up here? Isn't it easier when you get instructions on what to do and when to do it? Who wouldn't like having the answers before the exam?

But no book can give you the "right" answers or tell you how or what to feel. Instead, this book tries to provide comfort for you. You can read and experience it at your own pace. You can apply creative solutions for your grief in your own way.

Think of this book as a grief map. It helps you to see the path, but it can't tell you where to go.

The book is divided into chapters to give it a structure, but whatever you do, don't feel glued to the order. As in life, there is no set order to the many elements of grief. The only thing that's certain is that ideas may overlap, feelings may get turned inside out, and there will be contradictions.

Read passages marked THE DOCTOR IS IN to get suggestions based on Dr. Lister's years of grief counseling and on her personal experiences with death. Passages marked TRY THIS suggest journal-writing exercises, visualizations, and other creative or artistic ways for you to express yourself in the midst of grief, alone, and with your family and friends. Interesting facts about different cultures and religions show you how other people grieve, as do firsthand accounts of grief from other teens. Their poems, songs, and letters share questions, answers, and memories about people who have died.

You are definitely *not* alone.

As you read, remember the one you loved — but remember *you*, too. Grief involves letting go of someone who has died, but it also about holding on and recognizing life, especially your own. This book can help you to see that.

Grief may feel scary or terrible right now, but please remember that fear is temporary. This book will try to make things *less* scary. This is a new you, dealing with a new situation. These are new feelings. You will survive this.

Grief is not an ending. It is a beginning.

Start here.

I used to have a handle on life. Then it broke.

— Bumper Sticker

I
Understanding

The meaning of things does not lie in the things themselves, but our understanding of them.

— Antoine de Saint-Exupéry

When someone you love dies, you need to understand how this could have happened. How are you supposed to act, respond, or feel? What is the meaning of life and death? Why is grief such hard work?

Understanding what has happened is not always easy. You are looking at grief through a kaleidoscope made up of many shifting colors and shapes that change not just in the context of your teen life, but in the context of religious and cultural traditions and what other people think and feel.

The path to understanding lies *inside* of you. In time, the colors and shapes will begin to make more sense.

Chapter 1

Death and Life

You would know the secret of death?
But how shall you find it unless you seek it in
the heart of life?

— Kahlil Gibran

Are We In a State of Denial?

The bad news of death is *everywhere*.

News broadcasts deliver late-breaking reports: "Dozens perish in hurricane" or "Three children shot at school recess." Movies and video games blast us with bullets and bombs. On television, real-life crime and death are carried by all the major networks. Statistics quoted in the *Journal of the American Medical Association* say that you witness at least two murders on television every day. There's even an Internet web site called "Death Clock," where you can look up the estimated time of your own demise.

In our culture, whether we like it or not, death appears in Technicolor 24/7. But we don't like talking about it. When it happens close to home, many of us avoid the subject. A lot of people are uncomfortable even saying the word *death*. Incredibly, we've invented an entire vocabulary to describe death without using the actual word.

Expressions We Use
Instead of Saying a Person Died

Dropped the body	No longer with us	Departed
Six feet under	Expired	It's curtains
Bought the farm	Rest in peace	Croaked
Asleep	Gave up the ghost	With the angels now
Passed on	Ended it all	Kicked the bucket
Crossed over	Laid to rest	Checked out
Met the maker	Gone home	Has left us

A hundred years ago, teenagers understood and dealt with death very differently than they do today. In their own homes many people prepared bodies for burial. A relative's body was placed on the kitchen table, not placed on display in a funeral parlor. Elaborate customs and rituals to deal with death were a part of people's lives. They not only talked about death; early in their mourning process, they literally *lived* with a dead body.

So what's changed for today's teens? What's different for *you*?

Today, as we enter the twenty-first century, we are living in a strange state of death denial. You'd think we should be *more* publicly and privately enlightened about the experience and emotions of death than our ancestors were, but unfortunately this isn't the case. More often than not, adults may say, "You're just a teenager. Why should you worry about dying?" They think, "You have your whole life ahead of you." If someone in your life is dying, a parent or family member may keep facts hidden from you rather than discuss the truth. Then, when someone does die, no one knows what to say to you or to anyone else experiencing deep grief.

Our culture keeps death at a distance. Television shows us strangers real and imagined who die. We turn the channel and say, "Well, that just won't happen to *us*." In many ways we are so distracted by movies or video games that we've lost touch with what *real* death means in our *real* lives.

Not only are we in a state of death-denial, but we are also in a state of death-defiance. We defy death to find us as we stand behind our high-tech medical advances and extreme sports competitions. On some levels we have let the excitement of technology overshadow our humanness. We are no longer vulnerable in the same human way people were years ago. We have been desensitized.

But the fact is that death happens — *every day*.

We need the tools and words not to mask it or protect ourselves from it but to help us move through it as we continue to live. We need to pack our bags, pull out that map, and get out of the state of denial *immediately*.

When a person is born, we rejoice, and when they're married, we jubilate, but when they die, we pretend that nothing happened.

— Margaret Mead

YOUR GRIEF JOURNAL

As you move through the chapters of this book, you will be asking yourself questions and tossing around new ideas. Sometimes it helps to keep a record of those thoughts.

Go to the stationery store and find a journal that reminds you of the person who died. Is it his or her favorite color? Does it have a pretty picture on it? Is it big or small? This will be your Grief Journal.

Now select a pen, marker, or pencil that person would have liked. Write on the inside front cover: *I survive. I grieve. I love.* Write the name of the person who has died under that. The two of you will share this diary.

Some writers like lined pages, others do not. Sometimes you may choose to write in different colors or to draw when words don't come. Consider keeping several pens or pencils of different colors nearby should your mood change. Maybe you will write in one color to express your thoughts and use another color to express the thoughts of the person who has died.

Your Grief Journal is not a day-to-day record of what you do. It is a look at how your inner life is holding up in the face of grief. It is an exploration of how one person's death will ultimately change your life. Date each entry so you can chart your growth and progress.

The French writer Anaïs Nin, who began keeping journals in her childhood, described the process of daily journaling: "I chose the event of the day that I felt most strongly about, the most vivid one, the warmest one, the nearest one, the strongest one."

You should do the same.

Remember to keep your journal in a safe, private place. It is for your eyes only.

What Is Death to You?

O darkness! O in vain!
O I am very sick and sorrowful.

O brown halo in the sky near the moon, drooping
upon the sea!
O troubled reflection in the sea!
O throat! O throbbing heart!
And I singing uselessly, uselessly all the night.

— from "Out of the Cradle Endlessly Rocking"
by Walt Whitman

Begin the grief process by taking a look at your own associations with death. This doesn't have to mean looking at specific connections to the person who just died but at death in general. What are your basic feelings and beliefs? Can you define, even in a small way, what that word means to you?

Does the idea of death reduce you to tears, leave you in a panic, or is it very, very quiet?

Is death a hot, pounding sun, or is it a pelting rain?

Is death a constant intrusion, or is it uncommon in your neighborhood?

What is different about the death of a friend as compared to the death of a stranger, miles from where you live?

Is death more about forgetting or remembering?

Is death a black hole, or is it a ship passing onto a new shore?

I am standing upon the seashore. A ship at my
side spreads her white sails in the morning breeze
and starts for the blue ocean. She is an object of

7

beauty and strength and I stand and watch her until at length she is only a ribbon of white cloud just where the sea and sky come to mingle with each other. Then someone at my side says, "There! She's gone!"

Gone where? Gone from my sight — that is all. She is just as large in mast and hull and spar as she was when she left my side, and just as able to bear her load of living freight to the place of destination. Her diminished size is in me, not in her, and just at the moment when someone says, "There! She's gone!" there are other voices ready to take up the glad shout, "There! She comes!" and that is dying.

— Cathy Hainer, cancer patient, quoting
"A Parable of Immortality," by Henry Van
Dyke. The passage appeared in Cathy
Hainer's series of personal journals
excerpted in *USA Today* in 1999

Think about how your perception of death changes depending upon how often you come into contact with it. What shapes your definition of death *right now*?

VISUALIZATION

Close your eyes for a moment and visualize death as passage aboard a ship at sea. Is it cloudy or is the sun shining? Who is there?

Now, try to see death like rain falling against your face. What does that rain feel like? What other images come to mind when you think of dying and death?

Often we think of death as blackness, darkness, or an end. How do you respond to those images?

Try to think of death in terms of *all* your senses: sight, sound, touch, taste, and smell. Think about it not only as a going but as a *becoming*.

Write down the words and pictures that come to mind when you define death. You can make a list or doodle. Just try to get it down on the pages of your Grief Journal. These initial responses will be important for you to reread as you move through the continuing stages of grief.

What is the meaning of life? . . . The great revelation . . . never did come. Instead there were little daily miracles, illuminations, matches struck unexpectedly in the dark.

— Virginia Woolf

What Is Life to You?

Because we do not know when we will die, we get to think of life as an inexhaustible well. And yet everything happens only a certain number of times; and a very small number really. How many times will you remember a certain afternoon of your childhood; an afternoon that is so deeply a part of your being that you can't even conceive of your life without it? Perhaps four or five times more? Perhaps not even that. How many more times will you watch the full moon rise? Perhaps, twenty. And yet it all seems limitless.

— From *The Sheltering Sky* by Paul
Bowles. Brandon Lee quoted this passage
in his final interview before being killed
on the set of the movie *The Crow*

To understand the meaning of life, think about it in the broadest terms. Seek definitions for life that seem out of the ordinary.

What is life's temperature — hot, cold, or lukewarm?

What is life's driving purpose — to keep up that B average, get on the hockey team, or get a date to the prom?

Compare life now to when you were younger. When you were an infant, perhaps life was getting a hug, playing with blocks, and going for a ride in the stroller. Right now, average life may include school, tests, your boyfriend or girlfriend, or your new job.

Now, go a step further.

Define life *after* death — that is, *your* life after the death of someone you loved.

We typically think that life after death refers to heaven or the great beyond. But what if the real life after death is *yours*?

10

After all, you're the one who goes on living. We are sometimes so focused on the death part of grief that we may neglect to see that grief is really about life, *your* life.

The Doctor Is In

Life without the person who has died may feel like a crisis. But that does not mean you are doomed. In fact, the opposite is true.

Believe it or not, there is a symbolic connection between crisis and life. The Chinese symbol for crisis also means opportunity.

Did you ever think grief would present itself as an opportunity?

Life Cycles

Remember when your parents or teacher would talk about leaves falling from a tree as a metaphor for life and death? Leaves change colors and die and fall from the trees, but the old leaves feed the soil, and then — amazingly — green buds appear again in the springtime. This demonstrates how these powerful forces work together to keep planet Earth in business. The same is true with butterflies. The stages of transformation from caterpillar to chrysalis to butterfly show us life and death working in sync.

These processes happen *together*, in a natural cycle.

One day a gray-haired caterpillar hanging upside down on a branch surprised her. He seemed caught in some hairy stuff.

11

*"You seem in trouble," [Yellow the caterpillar]
said. "Can I help?"*

*"No, my dear, I have to do this to become a
butterfly."*

Her whole insides leapt.

*"Butterfly — that word," she thought. "Tell
me, sir, what is a butterfly?"*

*"It is what you are meant to become. It flies
with beautiful wings and joins earth to heaven. It
drinks only nectar from the flowers and carries the
seeds of love from one flower to another.*

*"Without butterflies, the world would soon
have few flowers."*

*"It can't be true!" gasped Yellow. "How can I
believe there's a butterfly inside you or me when all
I see is a fuzzy worm?*

*"How does one become a butterfly?" she asked
pensively.*

*"You must be willing to fly around so much
that you are willing to give up being a caterpillar."*

*"You mean to die?" asked Yellow, remember-
ing the three who fell out of the sky.*

*"Yes and no," he answered. "What looks like
you will die, but what's really you will still live.
Life is changed, not taken away. Isn't that different
from those who die without ever becoming butterflies?"*

— from *Hope for the Flowers* by Trina Paulus

As you begin to grieve, remember that life and death are both parts of a great cosmic process. The person who died was a part of that process. You are a part of that process. A new baby being born is also a part of that process.

Life cycles are about movement and flow — and change. You don't move *past* one thing to get to the other; you move *through* both.

The purpose of your grief right now is not to push *any* feelings away, especially not the uncomfortable ones. This grief here and now means going *through* every emotion, examining, questioning, and experiencing death and life together.

What we call the beginning is often an end.
And to make an end is to make a beginning.
The end is where we start from.

— T. S. Eliot

Try This:

NOW AND THEN

Look at cycles in your own life.

Take a piece of paper or use one of the pages in your Grief Journal.

On the left side of the page, quickly fill in what life is like now, immediately following the person's death. Don't think too much about this exercise. Just write whatever comes into your mind, as soon as you think of it.

Next, on the right side of your page, write down what life was like *before* the person you loved died.

Are the two columns very different? How are they the same?

Life after Mom died is scary.	Life before Mom died was normal.
Life after my boyfriend died is cold.	Life before my boyfriend died was romantic.
Life after someone died is blue.	Life before someone died was yellow.

Start with these examples. Try to add to this list as you move through your grief.

We are healed of a suffering only by experiencing it to the full.

— Marcel Proust

Chapter 2

Why It's Different for Teens

No one ever told me that grief felt so like fear. I am not afraid, but the sensation is like being afraid. The same fluttering in the stomach, the same rest-lessness, the yawning. I keep on swallowing. . . .

There is sort of an invisible blanket between the world and me. I find it hard to take in what anyone says. Or perhaps, hard to want to take it in. It is so uninteresting. . . .

There are moments, most unexpectedly, when something inside me tries to assure me that I don't really mind so much, not so very much, after all. . . .

On the rebound one passes into tears and pathos. . . . But the bath of self-pity, the wallow, the loathsome sticky-sweet pleasure of indulging it — that disgusts me. . . .

And no one ever told me about the laziness of grief.

— from *A Grief Observed* by C. S. Lewis

There Is No Normal

If you're looking for a list of what's normal about grief, you'll be looking for a long time. There really is no "normal" about any of this grief stuff — only basic guidelines with fuzzy lines in between. You think you're fine — and then you start bawling. You think you're a wreck — but then you can't cry. Sometimes grief feels manageable, and other times it feels beyond control. There are no hard-and-fast rules or signs. It can change from day to day — or not at all.

Forever Lost
David Dexter, age 14, England

I am turning, I am whirling
Spinning through the endless space
When at last I can stop swirling
Once again I'll see her face

I know I'll never stop the chase
Pointless though it might well be
Her soul is gone, its beauty stolen
All I have is her sweet face

The waxy grinning mask of death
Settles down upon her lips
The lips which I, her one companion,
Never could bring myself to kiss

Now she's gone, my life is empty
No longer is there meaning there
But still my dreams are full of vision
Of her brown eyes, her flying hair

Only in the night I have her
Holding her tightly to my chest
And then she's gone, lost in the dark
As once again I start my quest

Never try to underestimate how much is going on inside you. Even if you can't see it or understand, it's probably there. Teenagers feel deeply. *Grieving* teenagers feel even more deeply. The one thing you can count on is the fact that your emotions will surprise you, challenge you, and amaze you when you least expect it.

During the teen years, you're juggling homework, dating, and your part-time job. Your body has been undergoing major physical changes, too, as your hair, skin, and body parts have been developing and growing. Your hormones may be running wilder than before — and your moods were already unpredictable enough. You try to guess the meaning of every gesture and message in a teacher's glance or your best friend's wink, but you can't seem to figure out what's what. You *have* to make the basketball team . . . or else. You have to turn in the feature for the school paper . . . or else. You have to get the starring role in the school play . . . NOW. And then someone dies.

Are you responsible for that, too? How are you supposed to deal with that?

Dearest Papa
Marcella, age 18, Canada

As I entered the room your body lay still
I said good-bye, you say I love you, I say I love you
I break down in tears, no longer may I hide
All the pain, all the sadness, I am hiding inside

As if a year and a half happened just yesterday
As I held your hand, strolling down the bay
Kissing you good night, waking you in the morn
Too bad the morn is only now filled with mourn

Perfect you definitely were not
You messed up my life but always fought
Make good what you could but never looked back
Never asked for me to cut you any slack

Acceptance we all gave, for love is unconditional
But no longer may my life ever be full
You are gone, I sit but here, wishing to hold your
hand
Wanting you to see me on that graduation stand

Never shall you see me marry, never shall you see
my children
You have left my life when my life is just about to
begin
Who will ever give my boyfriends the third degree
Or tell me that I should always just be me

Why'd you have to mess up your life so bad
Because of your past I no longer have a dad
I love you so much I want you here next to me
Can't I just once have a normal life? Can't I just
be?

Going to Extremes

The deeper that sorrow carves into your
being, the more joy you can contain.

— Kahlil Gibran

Do you sometimes feel invulnerable or invincible?
Before now, it was hard to image *anyone* dying in your life.
Maybe you said, "I'm only fifteen!" You ignored the possibility of death.

Maybe you went over the speed limit. You told yourself you could never crash.

Maybe you had unprotected sex. You figured nothing would ever happen to you.

You took risks because they were fun, you felt alive, you were getting attention, and it was hard to imagine the long-term consequences of any reckless behavior.

Now that someone has died, do you see things differently? If you don't, are other people around you passing judgment on your risky actions?

Please know that this book isn't about whether or not you *should* take risks. That's up to you. This is about what all that risk-taking can mean for you in the process of grieving, because it can mean a lot. Taking risks and riding so many emotional highs and lows are almost certain to make your teen grief experience that much more intense. *Everything* in your life has enormous significance right now. Throw death into the mix and — *ka-boom* — the intensity grows. How will you handle it all?

Which of the statements below apply to you right now? Are you going to extremes?

- I'm hiding my grief and sadness from my family.

- I can't tell my parents about my grief. They have enough to worry about.

- I won't grieve with my parents because they don't care how I feel.

- If I start to talk about my feelings of grief, I am afraid I will lose control.

- My parents will be embarrassed if I cry and act like a mess.

- I am not willing to look like a mess.

- I cannot stand being a survivor in this crazy world.
- I wish I had died, too. It should have been me who died.
- I want to have sex because it makes me feel close to someone.
- I can't handle all the violence and death in this world.
- The world will never, ever be the same.
- I don't have to worry about death right now. It's a long way off for me.
- I wish I had some answers about this.
- Nobody deserves to die.
- Why isn't the whole world stopping to deal with this?
- I can't believe my life is on hold for this.
- This is happening at a bad time for me.
- Why won't everyone just leave me alone so I can deal with this in my way?
- Is this really happening to me?
- Why is my life such a soap opera?

There are so many ways in which being a teen can distort your grief. Sometimes it *definitely* feels like a soap opera.

You want home, school, family, and friends to be your safe and stable places, but the only stability you know has been broken up by someone's death. Who wants to worry about life ending when it has barely begun?

You may feel caught in the middle between childhood and adulthood. You want to curl up on your pillow like a little kid, but you may simultaneously want to forge ahead like a mature adult.

You may feel caught in the middle between divorced parents or quarreling siblings or friends. You seek comfort, but what you get instead is more conflict.

You may feel caught in the middle between handling yourself or others and falling apart. But you are afraid of showing weakness, so you grin and bear it, denying how you really feel.

As teenagers, you and your friends may *look* like adults, so people may make the mistake of thinking that you have adult ways to cope. Of course, this may or may not be the case. How are you supposed to know what to do?

During this time, you may be on the verge of separating emotionally from your parents. Now you have to separate from the person who has died, too. Separation almost always causes some level of anxiety. And what if you have to turn to the parents you're rebelling against — for *support*?

People may assume that you have a built-in support system of parents or other family members to make grieving easier. But in fact, the deceased may be a member of that support system. Where does that leave *you*, when the person who normally comforts you is actually the one who has died?

People may assume that teens are comforted automatically by peers. But when it comes to death, some friends just don't get it. They say it's uncomfortable not to understand something, so it's better just to stay away. Unless a friend has experienced grief firsthand, he or she might tune out when it comes to the subject of loss. Ironically, in your time of greatest need, your close friends may be missing in action. They're going to extremes, too — in the extreme *opposite* direction.

The Doctor Is In

There are differences in the way children, teens, and adults grieve.

Adults may seem better at preparing for and handling grief only because they've experienced death before. Maybe you, as a teen, have *not*.

Try not to underestimate your vulnerability, no matter what age you are. You may think you can handle anything and everything, but that may not be true. Even though you may understand more than younger children do, your pain, fear, and feelings of abandonment can still be strong and raw.

Pain is a part of being alive, and we need to learn that. Pain does not last forever, nor is it necessarily unbearable, and we need to be taught that.

— Rabbi Harold Kushner

Reality Checks

As a teen, you're on a mission to find yourself. You're trying new things, meeting new people, and diving headfirst into life. Try not to shelve these qualities when someone dies. You need to stay true to your version of reality, even when it astounds you. You need to stay true to it *especially* when it astounds you.

Reality check: You do not need to stop being a teenager in order to grieve. The opposite is true. Exactly what makes you unique as a teen is what makes your grief so powerful. Stay true to yourself when grieving.

Sometimes what comes up during grief are selfish needs and desires. You need to realize that it isn't necessarily a bad thing to be selfish in the middle of your mourning. Sometimes you may become focused on how death has interfered with *your* needs and schedules rather than worrying about the person who has died.

Reality check: In order to survive grief, you may need to focus on yourself instead of focusing on someone else.

Sometimes the only way to get the attention and affection you need is to ask for it. You may have to remind the people around you that they *shouldn't* stay away just because you're unpredictable. You need to help others get you through this. You are at a point in life when you'll do anything for independence, but teen grief often means telling people what you need and what you don't need. Or it means telling them that you don't know what you need. Tell them something, however, so they can support you.

IN THE MIRROR

Take a *visual* reality check right now. Look into a mirror. What do you see?

Remind yourself that *whatever* reality you see is fine.

Take a few moments to breathe deeply while holding your own gaze.

Have you been crying? Do you look good today? Are you tired? When you are worried about what and how you are *feeling*, get into your body for just a moment. Sometimes we let our thoughts overwhelm us. So stop thinking. Start looking.

What has changed in your looks since the person you loved died? You don't have to answer these questions in writing if you don't want to. Just take a moment with yourself to think carefully.

In order to face reality, you need to look at your real face — even with tired eyes, pimples and all. Just as no two fingerprints or snowflakes are the same, no two grieving experiences are ever the same.

Can you see that in the mirror?

Sad soul, take comfort, nor forget that sunrise never failed us yet.

— Celia Layton Thaxter

Too Young For This
Ryan, age 17, New Jersey

My friend's house has one of those big, screened-in porches that are really nice in warm weather. His mom smells like I would imagine June Cleaver smelled. He has brothers and sisters and a Mustang. And two weeks ago, my friend overdosed on heroin and died.

I went to his wake on a Wednesday. I hugged his brother, sat down in a rigid folding chair, and cried. As I glanced around the room, I saw my friends. Death really is a surreal experience as it completely changes the landscape of your life. Those who would normally have provided me with a shoulder to cry on were slumped in chairs around me, their own shoulders sagging too much to be of any help. I felt completely lost.

A woman walked slowly by a large group of us sitting up against the wall. Surveying our crowd, of which the oldest of us was pushing twenty-four, she sighed to no one in particular, "You're just too young for this."

He was too young for this.

Another friend and I drove home in complete silence. The Alkaline Trio CD whispered hints of normalcy through the speakers, but I don't think either of us noticed. He pulled up in front of my house, and I gave him a hug and got out of the car.

I stepped out into the bright sunlight, which seemed blinding and threatening rather than inviting, and toward my home, which seemed anything but. A voice called out to me.

"Hey, younger-than-me!" I turned to face a short, skinny Keebler elf of a man strolling down the street, wearing his snow hat proudly in the near seventy-degree weather. "How are ya?" he wanted to know through his timeless smile.

Sifting through the wide variety of answers to such a question on such a day, I came up with, "Fine, thanks, yourself?"

"Great, just great. I'm seventy years old and feeling great. My friend, he turned ninety-six three days ago. I'll tell ya, it's walking that'll do it for ya. A walk a day and you'll still be able to do this at my age." At this point he bent down and slapped the ground with two fists, his knees straight. "Beautiful day out, isn't it? Yes, sir, I'm feeling great! And you, son, you take care of yourself and feel great, too!"

I think I murmured something along the lines of "Thanks, you too," before I entered my house. I found my couch and it was still soft and comfortable, and my cat's hair still glazed the left armrest where he liked to sit and watch the world pass by his window.

The sun poured in through that window and I welcomed it. It felt warm on my face and cast a familiar light on the living room. I rolled over and closed my eyes. The sunlight beat against the back of my neck, and again I cried.

My friend? The old man? Or did I cry again for me, because the pain of a life cut short and the miracle of one that still resonates into old age makes an equation larger than my ability to figure it out or even comprehend at all. What any of this means is beyond me, beyond us all.

The sun shone warmly on my face and dried my tears.

Chapter 3

The Role of Ritual in Your Grief

After a great pain a formal feeling comes —
The Nerves sit ceremonious, like Tombs —
The stiff Heart questions was it He, that bore,
And Yesterday, or Centuries before?

— Emily Dickinson

For centuries, cultures have been using rituals to cope with the aftermath of death. Actions and objects are able to express what seems impossible to communicate through words.

Years ago, Americans had symbols of grief that signaled to the world, "Attention! Person in mourning! Be sensitive!" Guns were fired during military salutes.

Men wore black armbands.

Black crepe wreaths were hung on the doors.

For rural farmers in the eighteenth century, a funeral was not a funeral unless it was a proper one. A family could go into debt trying to plan the right food, gifts, and drink. It was all or nothing when it came to death and grief rituals.

In the 1880s, women's etiquette books prescribed wearing the right clothes for grieving, from black crepe dresses and veils to black-trimmed handkerchiefs and black crepe bloomers. Women who lost their husbands were required to go through deep mourning and wear all black for a whole year. Even children had to undergo the same strict rules about dressing during the grieving process.

Formal rituals act as an essential link for us, connecting the past, present, and future of our grief. So much work throughout the grief process is done inside an individual's

27

mind and heart. This can often be a solitary place. Ritual reminds a griever that he or she is part of a larger consciousness and tradition. It creates a balance between what is within a person and what is outside that same person.

Rituals act out a familiar social order agreed upon by a group of people. Ritual can strengthen a commitment to culture and family. The meaning of life may be reaffirmed by simple acts. At a funeral, for example, you have the freedom and safety to express conflicting emotions and can get in touch with your spiritual side. During this ritual, a simple hug or handshake for the bereaved is considered a very personal ceremonial gesture, representing what cannot be expressed in words. Placing a wreath on a casket or shoveling earth onto a coffin in the grave are powerful rituals that emphasize the finality of death while giving onlookers a chance to participate.

In the midst of teen grief, you may feel disconnected from society's rituals or traditions in the same way that you may feel disconnected from other parts of life right now. How can you reconnect? Sometimes it helps to examine the traditions of those in your immediate world and beyond.

I remember the soprano
Fanning herself at the piano,

And the preacher looming large
Above me in his dark blue serge.

My shoes brought in the smell of clay
To mingle with the faint sachet

Of flowers sweating in their vases.
A stranger showed us to our places.

The stiff fan stirred in my mother's hand,
Air moved, but only when she fanned.

I wondered how could all her grief
Be squeezed into one small handkerchief.

There was a buzzing on the sill.
It stopped, and everything was still.

We bowed our head and closed our eyes
To the mercy of the flies.

— "First Death" by Donald Justice

Religious and Cultural Traditions

African-American (Southern)

Early in the twentieth century, a wake and service would take place at a funeral parlor, a church, or the home of the deceased. Everyone gathered to eat food cooked by family members and share memories of the deceased. After two days, there was a funeral procession. The hearse led cars of the deceased family to the cemetery. They were usually accompanied by a parade of jazz musicians.

Custom played a great role in the burial ceremony. Mourners believed that it was important for a dead person to be buried feet facing east. This allowed him or her to rise up on Judgment Day. Otherwise, the deceased person would remain in the crossroads of the world. Coins were placed on the eyes of the dead to keep them closed. Sometimes coins were also placed in the hands and around the grave site, as another token for admittance to the spirit world.

Ancient Egypt

In the ancient world of pharaohs like King Tutankhamen, bodies were treated with spices, herbs, and chemicals so that rather than decomposing they became mummies. Even sacred animals like cats were mummified. These processes comforted the living. They prepared the dead for a safe journey through the underworld into their next life. Mummy powder was later sold by apothecaries in the Middle Ages because it was said to have great power.

Buddhism

The Tibetan Book of the Dead is a travelogue and book of knowledge about the after-death state. The book describes how Tibetan Buddhists obtain enlightenment through meditation, calm concentration, and the energy of the universe. It says, "Imagine you are sending this blessing, the light of healing compassion to the enlightened beings, to your loved one who has died." The book is meant to be read by one master or spiritual friend to another who is dying.

When someone is dying in a Burmese home, monks come to comfort them. They chant verses, and the monks help the dead person's good energies to be released. As long as the body is present the spirit can benefit by these gifts, sermons, and chants. Once death occurs, some Buddhists follow an Indian custom of burning the body. The Buddha's body itself was cremated, and this set the example.

Christianity

According to the Holy Canons of the Church, the body of a deceased Christian must be returned to the earth: ashes to ashes, dust to dust. In some Christian religions, cremation is, however, expressly forbidden.

Roman Catholics and other groups may honor the dead at a wake, usually held at a funeral home. Before the funeral and burial, family and friends visit with the dead body, which is in a casket (sometimes open, sometimes closed). In Greek Orthodox ceremonies, the body is left in an open casket during the funeral service at the church.

The casket is put into a grave in a cemetery plot, with some kind of a marker or monument — often the image of the holy cross.

Islam

Funeral rites in Islam are exceedingly strict. People are allowed to grieve for their dead, but they must not wail or sob. That is considered un-Islamic. The maximum period of mourning for a woman is three days if the deceased is a close relation. A woman is allowed to mourn her husband for a longer period of time.

Preparation for burial starts with washing the deceased, a ceremony called *Ghusi*. The entire Muslim community participates, washing the body three times with soap and water. If any impurity has fallen on the body of the deceased, it must be removed. After being wrapped and/or perfumed (*Kafan*), prayers (*Salat*) begin. The Janazah prayer is read by the nearest relative. Then, after a funeral service in deference to Allah, the body is buried in a shallow grave. Women are allowed to visit the graveside, but only if they do not wail. Ending one's mourning represents an acceptance of Allah's verdict.

Judaism

Judaism marks mourning by a series of grieving ceremonies, from the exact moment of death onward. First and
foremost, tradition requires the daily recitation, for eleven
months following burial, of the mourners' Kaddish, a prayer
for parents, spouses, siblings, and children. This prayer is
spoken in honor of the dead. Interestingly, it does not mention death or grief, but instead focuses on life.

The Mourners' Kaddish,
Traditional Jewish Prayer

*Magnified and sanctified be Your
name, O God, throughout the
world, which You have created
according to Your will. May Your
sovereignty be accepted in our
own days, in our lives, and in the
life of all the House of Israel,
speedily and soon, and let us say
Amen. May your great name be
blessed forever and ever.*

A clear-cut, ritualized structure allows Jewish mourners to
open their hearts and openly express their sorrow as they move
on with life. The family's arrival at home after a funeral sets a
process in motion to take the family back into the world of the
living: the shivah. The immediate family of the deceased goes
through a seven-day period of mourning. Low stools are placed
around the room so the family can "sit shivah." All of the mirrors are covered so bad spirits cannot come into the room. The
covering of the mirrors also symbolizes the fact that mourners
are supposed to concentrate their thoughts on the person who
has died, rather than on themselves and their own appearances.

32

Native American

Each Native American tribe has unique customs, but most tribes are alike in the belief that the soul is set free by death. The funeral is a time to dress the dead in native clothing and celebrate the passage to the afterlife. Many Native American people have been known to predict the exact date and time they would die. One Ojibwa medicine man describes how old people go off alone when they know they are dying. Common custom dictates that the dying give away or make arrangements to give away everything before they die. That way there is nothing for anyone to fight over after death.

Navajo death custom has to do with fear. Fear leads them to destroy the house of the dead person, while relatives burn the body. After the burning ritual, they are careful to run away in a winding path so the dead person's spirit can't follow them. Even after death, Native Americans consider saying the dead person's name taboo. It is like calling the spirit back where it does not belong.

Native Americans believe that death is but a change from one state of being into another. They do not want to call a freed soul back. That soul must now soar to the Great Spirit and common creator.

Did You Know?

- Early Native Americans shot arrows into the air to drive spirits away.

- Mexicans drop marigold flowers on the streets to guide the dead back home during *el Día de los Muertos* (the Day of the Dead).

- Paper money and garments are burned as symbols on behalf of the dead in China.

- Sub-Saharan African families form a brightly colored funeral procession and hold open conversations with their departed loved ones.

- Aborigines burn their breasts and slash their faces in a brutal ritual after family members have died.

- In Japan, people make paper boats with lanterns and set them onto the water to carry away the soul of the devil.

- Jewish mourners slash a piece of their clothing to show how they are marked by death.

- Pygmies in the Congo pull down a dead person's hut on top of him and then move their camp away from the area.

- The Maori of New Zealand place dead people in huts that are later burned by mourners wearing wreaths of green leaves, yelling, and cutting themselves with knives. They continue the ritual a few years later when the bones are cleaned, covered in red earth, and put in a special cave.

- In northern Siberia, the Chukchee keep a three-day silent watch over the dead body to make sure the soul has departed.

One of the most important things to remember about rituals, no matter what cultural or religious tradition they are based in, is that they are not just for the dead. They're for the living. Food offerings and other cultural traditions show people's humanity. Rituals bring together different generations, different classes, and different points of view. They are yet another reminder that we *all* experience death, we *all* live with death, and we *all* mourn death.

Try This:

MAKE UP A RITUAL

Think about how your own cultural and geographic background is affecting your grief process. Do you know what rituals and ceremonies are celebrated in your family?

In your Grief Journal, make up a unique, new funeral ritual for the person who has died. Where would you host it? What music would you choose? Who would attend? Who would participate?

The centerpiece of your ritual should be a tribute to the person who has died. You don't need to write someone's life story. Tell the best parts. How are you connected to the person who died? What made the person smile? Identify at least three ways in which this person's life impacted yours.

Be sure that your ritual honors the things the person who died liked best.

Truly, it is in the darkness that one finds the light, so when we are in sorrow then this light is nearest to all of us.

— Meister Eckhart

II
Feeling

The heart is forever inexperienced.

— Henry David Thoreau

*F*eeling is the fuel that takes us from one place to another, through all stages of grief, from the beginning to the moment we realize we need to let grief go. It is present in the mind, spirit, *and* the body.

No matter what we try to anticipate in the grieving process, our emotions may take over unexpectedly.

Right now you may feel "deadened" by this experience. But all of your feeling is a confirmation that in the middle of grief and sorrow, you are still very much alive.

Chapter 4

Step by Step

Turn your stumbling blocks into
stepping-stones.

— Anonymous

Expert psychologist Elisabeth Kubler-Ross wrote many books about death and bereavement. In her most famous text, *On Death and Dying,* she names five specific stages that everyone experiences when they are either dying or grieving:

1. Denial and isolation
2. Anger
3. Bargaining
4. Depression
5. Acceptance

In her preface to the book, Kubler-Ross says that after going through each of the stages we "will learn much about the functioning of the human mind, the unique human aspects of our existence, and will emerge from the experience enriched and perhaps with fewer anxieties about (our) own finality." She believes that the stages are the essential way to experience and understand grief. They are a way to see yourself and your relationship to life and death in sharper focus. Of course, stages are merely one model for grief. There are varied theories on why and how grief happens.

Psychoanalyst Sigmund Freud looked at grief in a slightly different way but with as much impact. In *Mourning and*

Melancholia, he talks about "griefwork" in relation to personal connections. He believed that forging emotional attachments (he called this cathexis) was a process that needed to be done in reverse when grieving (he called this decathexis). Freud's theories say that griefwork is about letting go of an old connection by making a new identity for yourself in which the dead person is not present.

The Doctor Is In

Imagine landing on the island of Lilliput in *Gulliver's Travels*, where you are soon captured by the miniature Lilliputians who tie you down to the ground with a hundred ropes. Now imagine the process of grief as a cutting off of each one, rope by rope.

As each cord is cut, you get a bit of your own life's energy back. Each rope that is removed is symbolic of another stage of grief experienced and conquered.

But remember: Just because you are cutting ties does not mean you are turning your back on or forgetting the person who has died.

Whether it's Freud or Kubler-Ross, therapist or priest, teacher or parent, different people may offer you different theories of grief. As you experience the feelings (and lack of feelings) surrounding the grief experience, you may be expected to understand and process a lot of information. Chances are that you can never *fully* prepare for the kinds of changes this loss will make in your daily life.

The night I lost you
someone pointed me towards
the Five Stages of Grief.
Go that way, they said,
it's easy, like learning to climb
stairs after the amputation.
And so I climbed.
Denial was first.
I sat down at breakfast
carefully setting the table
for two. I passed you the toast —
you sat there. I passed
you the paper — you hid
behind it.
Anger seemed more familiar.
I burned the toast, snatched
the paper and read the headlines myself.
But they mentioned your departure,
and so I moved on to
Bargaining. What could I exchange
for you? The silence
after storms? My typing fingers?
Before I could decide, Depression
came puffing up, a poor relation
its suitcase tied together
with string. In the suitcase
were bandages for the eyes
and bottles of sleep. I slid
all the way down the stairs
feeling nothing.
And all the time Hope
flashed on and off
in defective neon.
Hope was a signpost pointing
straight in the air.

41

Hope was my uncle's middle name,
he died of it.
After a year I am still climbing,
though my feet slip
on your stone face.
The treeline
has long since disappeared;
green is a color
I have forgotten.
But now I see what I am climbing
towards: Acceptance
written in capital letters,
a special headline;
Acceptance,
its name in lights.
I struggle on,
waving and shouting.
Below, my whole life spreads its surf,
all the landscapes I've ever known
or dreamed of. Below
a fish jumps: the pulse
in your neck.
Acceptance. *I finally*
reach it.
But something is wrong.
Grief is a circular staircase.
I have lost you.

— "The Five Stages of Grief" by Linda Pastan

It's Up to You

Grief may happen for you in stages or not in a linear way at all. There's no confirmed starting line or finish line. In fact, you may be overwhelmed by all the facts and ideas.

What you *can* do is pay attention to changes in yourself.

Consider those changes your stages. Whether they come rushing in all at once or take weeks to evolve, they are happening at the right pace for you. Remind yourself that this grief is what you make it. Identifying changes and "stages" helps us to explain what's going on. It lets us understand and feel at the same time.

We grieve in a variety of ways, but there are no guarantees about what, when, why, or how anything will happen. Nothing says for sure that you will experience grief in the same way as your friend or family member. You may linger longer in some stages than others or skip some stages altogether.

Since the grief experience is typically painful, you want to know how long it will last, but there are no definite answers to that question, either. It takes as long as it takes for you to work your way through your own vast range of emotions.

The only thing that is proven is if you start with small steps, soon you will be making big leaps. In time, you will see your way through.

I need the thing that happens when your brain shuts off and your heart turns on.

— from *Prozac Nation* by Elizabeth Wurtzel

WHAT OTHER PEOPLE SAY

Take out your Grief Journal. Over time, people have developed their own rules about the stages and experiences of grieving. Sometimes it is useful for you to look at what kinds of rules people in your family or inner circle have been promoting to you.

On the top of a clean page in your journal, write the words WHAT OTHER PEOPLE SAY TO ME ABOUT GRIEF AND MOURNING.

Now make a list of all the things people have told you.

Did anyone tell you to dress a certain way at the memorial — like in black?

Did anyone tell you to behave a certain way — like "Don't cry in public?"

What did people say to comfort you the first week after someone has died? What are they saying a month later?

List the words people use to describe their own experiences with grief. Do you get any conflicting messages?

Put an asterisk next to the things you believe are true.

Cross off the things you do not believe.

Chapter 5

Your Responses and Emotions

Color of Grief
Venetia, age 15, Texas

I see it now.
A mixture of colors.
A confusion of feelings.
Some are bright,
Like the redness of anger,
Some are bold,
Like the blackness of confusion.
Some are plain to see,
Like the whiteness of sadness.
Some are in between,
Like a rainbow of madness.
Yet they now run together,
A drab, gray puddle.
The only way to see my grief
Is to look into my puddle.

Note: Venetia wrote this poem after the death of her seventeen-year-old friend John. Six months after she wrote it, she died in a car accident.

The different emotions of grief make up a rainbow. There are as many colors in grief as there are moods and feelings.

Do you feel frozen? Grumpy? Tense? Sleepless? Hyper?

Let yourself be scrambled. Feel stuck for now. Feeling out of control may be exactly the right place for you.

The Doctor Is In

When you have many responses and emotions happening at once, you may experience a sudden preoccupation with the person who has died. You're experiencing memory and fantasy of the dead person through a veil of emotion. Thoughts are constant, while actions and feelings may be less predictable.

Try not to be self-conscious about it.

Try not to fight your feelings one by one.

As emotions flow out, pay attention. Accept them as they come, in whatever order they come, just as you've accepted other aspects of grieving up to this point.

Emotional Checklist

Go through this list and think about all the items that apply to you. There's a chance that you may actually feel *all* of these emotions in a single afternoon. Don't be intimidated by your sudden flood of feeling or by feeling nothing at all. It happens. It won't be this overwhelming forever.

What do you feel?

❑ Empty
❑ Sad
❑ Mad
❑ Euphoric
❑ Withdrawn
❑ Worried
❑ Silly

❑ Pining
❑ Anxious
❑ Helpless
❑ Suicidal
❑ In need of wisdom
❑ A surge in creativity
❑ Disbelief

- ❏ Like nothing
- ❏ Preoccupied
- ❏ Paranoid
- ❏ Like you cannot sleep
- ❏ Indecisive
- ❏ Abandoned
- ❏ Judged
- ❏ Like you don't belong
- ❏ Idealistic
- ❏ There is no God.

- ❏ There is *only* God.
- ❏ Like you must forgive
- ❏ Extremely doubtful
- ❏ Extremely optimistic
- ❏ Curious
- ❏ Weak
- ❏ Like a different person
- ❏ Afraid
- ❏ Resigned
- ❏ Like fighting

Try This:

RAINBOW

Did you know that different colors signify mourning in different locations in the world?

- Ancient Greek and Roman Empires believed that the color BLACK symbolized the dark gloom of mourning. People in the United States and Europe also think of black as the color of death.

- In Ethiopia, the color GRAYISH BROWN signifies the color of the earth where the dead return.

- In Thailand and Turkey, people mourn with the color PURPLE, which symbolizes royalty.

- Persia (now Iran) once mourned with PALE BROWN because it was the color of withered leaves.

- People of the South Sea Islands wore BLACK-and-

WHITE stripes when mourning, to represent both sorrow and hope happening at the same time.

- The people of South Africa associate the color RED — the color of blood and death — with mourning.

- In China, people mourn with the color WHITE, because it is the emblem of hope.

- In Egypt, people consider the color YELLOW important for grief because it is the color of dead and dying leaves. Some also consider it the color of exaltation.

- The people of Syria, Armenia, and other Mideast nations consider the color BLUE important in mourning, especially SKY BLUE. This represents the hope that the deceased has gone to the skies, or heaven.

What is the color of *your* grief? Does it change when you're mad, sad, or happy? Describe why you picked this color. Write more about it in your Grief Journal.

As you proceed through your grief, remember that there is no right or wrong order in which to feel or experience its many colors and moods. Each stage has its own personality and its own consequences. You may experience one, none, or all of the stages.

Try to remember at all times, under all conditions, that the rules of grief are yours to make — or to break.

Shock

Death
Sarah, age 13, California

With a crash and a bang, she was thrown from the car through the windshield and run over by another car. She was killed instantly.

The morning that we got the call was just like any other morning. It was Sunday, Father's Day, in fact, and it was about 7:00 A.M. My sister and I were getting our presents ready for our dad when the phone rang. Like always, my sister and I ran to the phone. The phone call was for our parents. It was my sister's godfather, Paul. I handed the phone to my parents, and I stood outside the room eavesdropping.

"Hi, Paul," said my mom. "Oh, my God," she continued.

My dad was very impatient and kept saying "What? What?" Then my mom finally blurted out the words.

"Danielle's been killed in a car accident."

My heart stopped. It felt like someone reached into my chest and pulled out my heart.

That afternoon around 1:00 P.M., we went to my sister's godparents' house to comfort them. When we reached the house, I felt kind of strange. My feelings were so jumbled, I just couldn't think straight. I was shocked and angry.

There were a lot of people at the house. Most of them were Danielle's friends. People who were there were crying and sobbing, even macho guys. I couldn't cry then, even though I knew it was okay.

I know I talk a lot, but that day, then and there, I didn't talk at all. I felt like someone pulled out my stomach, tied a knot in it, and stuck it back in. In other words, I felt like I was going to throw up. The only sounds that filled the house were silence and a few sobs which the breeze carried out the windows.

I walked into Danielle's room, and it was only filled with more sadness and anger. I left. I walked slowly into the kitchen, grabbed a soda, and sat down to think. I could still not understand why God had to take a life so young. I did not want to be alone. I walked into the living room. There sat my mom and dad on one couch with Danielle's parents. They looked uneasy. I never saw them like this before, all four adults just sitting there, staring. I wanted to break the silence but I didn't know how. I really wanted very much to go home.

On the way home, I stared out the window, not knowing if I should talk. I finally said, "Why her?"

That day I remember so vividly, it is like a picture on my living room wall — it certainly has stuck in my mind.

The first sensation you may become aware of when you hear someone has died is shock, almost no feeling at all. You're empty. Numb. Frozen. Stuck. It's like your body is protecting you for a while, shutting down until you are ready to process the death that has occurred.

Being numb is like wearing a blanket over your head. It dulls your senses and your responses to your situation. You act like a robot. People look at you strangely, and maybe they even get annoyed by the fact that you are constantly "zoned out." You don't know what to say anymore, so you don't talk at all.

Where were you when you got the news that someone died? That moment has a big impact on your thoughts and memories and on the patterns of your grief. The impact of the moment is what brought on the numbness. It may also be what takes you to other places in grief, too.

50

Sometimes when we feel numb, it's as if we've lost the capability to feel anything. You may even feel bad because it seems like you're not sad and not grieving. But you *are* grieving. You need to trust that.

Even if you feel like *you* are the one who died, try to remember that you are still very much alive. Consider yourself in hibernation for the time being. Know that grief takes time and you are at the very beginning of the process. You will feel numb, but try not to close off completely. Know from the very start that you *can* master your understanding of grief.

Try This:

FOCUS ON THE FACTS

Try to take a step back from the intensity of your situation. You've established that you probably can't control your responses to the death. But what you *can* control is your awareness of what's happening.

It sounds weird, but when you take a moment to step back and examine facts instead of feelings, you can actually help your emotions to get back on track. You sharpen your senses with precise detail. That makes your head clear up and lets feelings flow better. You move from shock and numbness into other stages of grieving.

Start a habit of keeping track of the grief stages in your Grief Journal.

Clear the fog inside your head by making a list of everything you've been eating, what homework you've done, who you've hung out with, how you've been sleeping, and other things since you learned of the death.

Lists can help you get grounded. Focus on the facts.

Denial

You have learned something. That always
feels at first as if you had lost something.

— George Bernard Shaw

Numbness may be followed by intense feelings of denial. You might pretend that death and grief are not happening. This is not to say that you're losing your grip on reality — just that your own protective barriers are coming up.

We're amazing creatures. In many ways, denial is a force field that hums around us after a death. Somewhere inside, we're readying ourselves for the harder work of grieving and adapting to life without the person we've lost. We put up the denial shield so we can absorb the events surrounding a death.

Yet although denial is, in part, a natural process, it should be short-lived, and you need to help it pass. Listen to the ways in which you might demonstrate the denial.

Do any of these apply to your experiences?

- You talk about the dead person as if he or she is still alive.

- You see someone walking down the street and momentarily mistake him or her for the dead person.

- You pretend that the person who died is away on a vacation, you are convinced that he or she is still coming back.

- You won't move or disturb the person's belongings, and you get very upset if anyone else disturbs them.

- The minute the person dies, you get rid of all articles and memories of that person.

- You start a literal search for the deceased. You may search for a friend in her classroom or by her locker. You may look for a dead parent at home.

- You immerse yourself in your schoolwork, after-school activities, or job to the exclusion of everyone and everything else.

- You turn to drugs, alcohol, or sex rather than deal with your pain and feelings.

Try not to worry if any of the above statements reflect your state of mind. Almost everyone experiences denial of some kind, especially when you lose someone who is very close to you.

Try not to be afraid of your thoughts. After someone dies, you may find yourself thinking about the dead person a lot. You also may find out that you aren't thinking about the dead person at all. Either response may be a part of the process.

Try not to overreact. Don't cut up all your photos of the person when you are numb. You may want them later. The important thing to remember here is not to do anything immediately. Your feelings are likely to change more than once. Don't do something you won't be able to take back, like destroying objects that remind you of the person.

Try not to let yourself numb the numbness. Sure, alcohol and drugs might help you feel calmer for a little while, but all you are doing is running away from one problem into the arms of another. If you are drinking or smoking pot to excess after someone dies, definitely go talk to someone about it.

Denial may seem like a safer place to be, but try not to hide there. A time *will* come when you will want to know your feelings.

The Doctor Is In

In the process of denial, a search for a dead person is not unusual. You may drive past someone's favorite park or restaurant or any place that reminds you of him or her. It is perfectly natural to want to see the person again. Likewise, you may find yourself talking aloud to someone who has died.

All this means is that you probably want to talk. You miss the person.

If your conversations continue to the point where your regular routines and relationships get disrupted, *that*'s when you need to let a parent, friend, or therapist help you understand what's going on.

I've been wondering if all the things I've seen
Were ever real, were ever really happening.

— from "Everyday Is a Winding Road"
by Sheryl Crow

Wondering

There ain't no answer.
There ain't gonna be any answer.
There never has been an answer.
That's the answer.

— Gertrude Stein

You made it through the shock. You survived denial. But what do you do when your thoughts start racing? What if things *still* make no sense? Or, what if grief slams you with no feeling at all?

You may find yourself transforming into something of a grief thinker, not a doer.

That's when the questioning begins. *Why did this person have to die? Why is this happening to me? When is this going to end?*

You're looking for answers and justification for the death. The unfortunate thing about dealing with grief is that we can ask a million questions and we may never get a single answer. We certainly may not get answers to satisfy us.

The Doctor Is In

The process of questioning and wondering is crucial. But you need to prepare yourself for the fact that you may get no answers.

Grief is not about answers, it's about the asking.

55

Basic research is what I'm doing when I don't know what I'm doing.

— Wernher von Braun

You may start your wondering by questioning specific circumstances surrounding the death. *What happened — and why? Who did the person talk to before he or she died? Why were they in the wrong place at the wrong time?*

Next, you may look for someone to punish for what has happened. Who can you hold accountable for the death? *Is this death my fault? Who can I blame?*

Finally, you may turn to the universe for answers. *Why does someone so young have to die? How can God do this? What is the meaning of life?*

You may have this need to KNOW EVERYTHING.

You are sure that if you know things, you'll get over the grief faster.

WONDERING JAR

Take an empty bowl or jar or coffee can and turn it into your Wondering Jar.

Each time you feel haunted by a who, what, why, when, or how question, get it out of your head by writing the question on a scrap of paper and putting it into the jar. Don't let yourself get bogged down by your wondering. Let the questions come up — and then let them go, tossing them into the jar.

Remember: This is not about finding answers. It is all about the asking.

Questioning that goes on and on can affect everything.

Maybe you begin to second-guess day-to-day actions. You wonder about other things, like what you're doing at school and at home. You wonder what the repercussions will be if you do something risky. You look for relationships between events of all kinds, good and bad.

> *All we can say to someone is that vulnerability to death is one of the given conditions of life. We can't explain it any more than we can explain life itself. We can't control it or sometimes even postpone it. All we can do is try to rise beyond the question "Why did it happen?" and begin to ask the question "What do I do now that it has happened?"*
>
> — from *When Bad Things Happen to Good People* by Rabbi Harold Kushner

You may also grieve through other kinds of loss. If you lose a girlfriend or boyfriend, you may compare the breakup to death. These connections can help you break through and understand why and how you grieve.

Connections let you find your way back into your own life again.

Try This:

CHART YOUR LOSS

Create a chart in your Grief Journal that tracks different kinds of losses from your life.

You may see patterns of thoughts and feelings. Make a list of those painful things that have happened. What kind of loss causes the greatest or the least grief? Is it possible that losing something or someone can have a positive result?

Some of the experiences you might record include:

- Separation after parents' divorce
- Issues about adoption or foster care
- Fires, floods, and other dramatic events
- Financial setbacks for you or your family
- Getting suspended or kicked out of school
- Not getting on a sports team or into a club or group
- Having an argument with a good friend or relative
- Changing a love relationship
- Moving to a new home or school

- Contracting an illness or disease or living with some-one who is sick

In your journal, compare these other losses to what you are feeling now, after someone has died. Write down the ways in which the experiences are similar and different.

Are you feeling about your dad's death the same way you felt about breaking up with your girlfriend? Are you responding to your friend's death in the same way that you responded to the loss of your cat? And what if your cat's death was a more traumatic loss for you?

Try not to be alarmed if connections you make seem random. This is a natural part of the process.

What the hell am I doing
falling in love with pain again and again and
again and again . . .

— from "Road to Dead" by Paula Cole

Although you may tell yourself everything is cool as you move forward in the grief process, uncertainty is a painful thing to accept. All the wondering in the world may never get you any final answers. You may challenge the universe with questions time and again. Maybe you'll fight until someone gives you answers NOW.

But try not to fight. Try to let the uncertainty exist. It may be uncomfortable, but it is not toxic. What *is* toxic is hanging on to something you cannot control.

Try to focus on things you *can* control.

Ask your questions and keep moving through. You want to pass through this wondering stage of grief. You don't want to let the questioning hold you back from moving forward in your own life.

Guilt

When things go wrong, don't go with them.

— Anonymous

Without the satisfaction of knowing why, you may look for someone to blame. Someone like . . . *yourself*.

There are many reasons you can feel guilty.

You may actually have been directly responsible for the death.

What if you were driving under the influence and you got into a car accident on your street? What if your gun misfired and shot your friend? In these cases, you can point to specific moments where your actions literally caused a death, whether it was an accident or it was intentional. You may suffer pangs of backbreaking guilt about the event, and you will definitely need to talk to someone about how to move through it.

But guilt is not always as clear-cut and easy to identify.

There are other times when you will feel guilty because you *think* you must have done something wrong to cause the death. Or perhaps you think you didn't do enough to prevent the death. Survivor's guilt gnaws at you from the inside out, making you question your actions and doubt yourself. In many cases, you feel guilty because you didn't die, someone else did. You may also feel guilty because you're not perfect or because you can't be in two places at one time. (By the way: Can *anyone* do or be those things? No. Guilt can be unrealistic and demanding.)

The bitterest tears shed over graves are for
words left unsaid and deeds left undone.

— Harriet Beecher Stowe

One of the ways guilt reveals itself is through "what if?" questions. We tell ourselves things about the events preceding a person's death and take on blame as we do it. We say, "If only I had or hadn't done something."

If only . . . I had driven the car, and he had not.
If only . . . I had been there when it happened.
If only . . . I had spoken to my friend before she died.
If only . . . I had done something else.
If only . . . I had stayed in closer touch.
If only . . . I had been home when he called.
If only . . . I hadn't laughed when she said she wanted to talk.
If only . . . I had been a better friend.

It is impossible for any of us to rewrite the past, and statements like those above will probably succeed in making you feel more frustrated and sad. If you find yourself saying these words, try to stop. Make an effort to consciously change your thinking and speaking. There is nothing you can do to change the past, so why not put your energy in other directions? Try not to set yourself up for failure. Instead, focus on the future.

Like, what can you do right *now*?

Try This:
APOLOGY

When you feel guilty, you often wish you could apologize for something you did or didn't do.

So go ahead. Apologize to the person who has died.

Is there something you forgot to say to the deceased while he or she was still alive? Is there something you wish you'd never said? Are you sorry that the person suffered or felt pain? Be specific and personal. You can write this in your Grief Journal if you want, or you can write it onto a scrap of paper that you throw away.

Sometimes hanging on to this kind of apology keeps your guilt going.

Maybe you need to spit it out and then rip it up. Do what works.

The miserable have no other medicine,
But only hope.

— William Shakespeare

What is the difference between
GUILT and REGRET?

GUILT says,
"I didn't do enough." You diminish yourself when
you feel guilty.

REGRET says,
"I did the best I could." You may have made an
error, but you do not put yourself down.

Regret

To My Dearest Friend
Jessica, age 17, Minnesota

I miss you so much. I feel so alone without you. I loved you so much. You never knew how much I loved you. You were my best friend, but I always wished you were my boyfriend. I was afraid to tell you how I felt about you because I was afraid our friendship would be ruined. I now wish I would have told you about this because then I wouldn't be wondering how you would have responded after I told you. Maybe you felt the same but you were also afraid of what would happen to our friendship. I guess now I'll never know. Since I've lost you I've realized a few things: I loved you more than I ever thought I could love someone, and I also realize that I have to tell people how I am feeling in the future. I might never get the chance again. I have loved you and will always love you. You will be in my heart forever.

Regret is about things we wish we had done or said differently. You may feel disappointment and sorrow, but regret knows the past cannot be changed. Unlike guilt, it also knows that we cannot be blamed as bad. For example, we feel regret about not spending time with Grandma before she died, but instead of punishing ourselves with guilt and lingering on what is wrong with us, we volunteer to spend time with our remaining, living grandparents.

One of the ways regret reveals itself is through the act of wishing. We wish for a different past. At the same time, we are willing to make promises for a different future.

I wish . . . I had remembered your birthday last year.

I wish . . . we had taken that ski trip together.

I wish . . . we were still going out when you died.

I wish . . . the team had won the championship.

I wish . . . you hadn't suffered so much.

I wish . . . I had done the dishes last week when you asked
me to.

I wish . . . I hadn't rushed you off the phone last weekend.

I wish . . . you were here to hold me.

I wish . . . you were here so I could hold you.

The Doctor Is In

We tend to suffer through our guilt. We have the power
to learn from our regrets.

The difference is in the self-concept.

Has grief made you think better or worse of yourself?
Although they are different emotions, the best thing about
both guilt and regret is that they scream at us, "Pay attention to what is going on!" No matter which way they ar-
rive, both make us aware.

Don't forget that just a short time ago, you may have
been feeling numb and frozen, feeling nothing. Now you
have stepped inside guilt and regret. You're feeling *something* now. Don't sell yourself short. This awareness is
progress.

As I tell patients of all ages, maybe for the first time
you are beginning to see the possibility of a light at the end
of the tunnel. Dramatic emotions like these have overwhelmed your senses, but I can promise you the drama will
die down.

In time, you will be able to unburden yourself from the
guilt and the regret.

IF ONLY, I WISH

Open your Grief Journal. Are you ready to make lots of lists about your guilt *and* your regrets? Because guilt and regret can be like raw emotional nerves, this exercise may be difficult.

Look at the "If Only" and "I Wish" lists in this chapter. You may want to copy some of those examples if they apply to you. Write down specific "If Only" and "I Wish" lists that relate to your personal grieving experience.

Try to make the lists work for you by turning them into positive actions. When you say "If only I had listened," maybe add, "From now on, I will try to listen to my friends. I will send them more e-mails and sit with them at lunch tomorrow."

Specific things you promise to do may ease your grief and make you feel better about the future.

Whether you're feeling pounding guilt or wistful regret, you need to accept one important fact above all others: *Nothing* you feel or say will bring the dead person back. No matter how many times you apologize, that person is gone.

You can spend hours pondering whether you could have prevented this person's death, but you will *never* know for sure. Once you understand and accept that, it may be easier to move through wondering, guilt, or regret and explore some of the other aspects of grief.

How will you handle the unpredictable and complex world of your emotions?

Fears

*I'm not afraid to die, I just don't want to be
there when it happens.*

— Woody Allen

Being afraid in grief can mean many different things.
When someone close to you dies, you may become afraid of
your own mortality. You might also feel scared about the
effect death will have on your life.

*How will this death affect my other friendships? How
will this death change my family? How will this death change
me?*

Is someone else going to die now?

What about me? When am I going to die?

In the face of grief, you fear the worst. You know things
will never, ever be the same.

In time, you will find the strength to face those fears one
by one. For now, try to express yourself and get in touch
with exactly what it is that scares you. Find a safe place to do
this.

Try This:

SAFE PLACE

Just as your emotions are running wild and free, take
time to let your senses do the same. Oftentimes, a creative
visualization can relax the buzz in your brain. It can calm
your fears.

Close your eyes.

Think about a cozy place, preferably your favorite place. This must be a place where you feel safe. What are you doing there? What do you see?

In your mind, wrap yourself in blankets. Curl up under the bedsheets. Squeeze into the corner of your closet, the secret hiding place in your old house when you were a kid.

In your mind, sit very still.

If you are at home, consider turning the lights down low or lighting a candle. Scented candles are even better. Whenever you can enliven several senses at once, you will feel more contented and in touch with yourself.

Once you've visualized this comfort zone, save it. Remember it.

You may need to go to it again someday soon. Throughout the grief process, it may help to know where and how you can feel safe inside your own skin.

The fishermen know that the sea is
dangerous and the storm terrible, but they
have never found these dangers sufficient
reason for remaining ashore.

— Vincent van Gogh

Tears

*Life is made up of sobs, sniffles, and smiles,
with sniffles predominating.*

— from "The Gift of the Magi" by O. Henry

When you feel sadness and despair, you may cry. You could get quiet. You may feel depressed. Maybe you get nauseous. Everyone reacts differently.

We think despair equals tears only, but an emotional swing into sadness might affect your sleeping pattern. You might lose sleep or sleep too much. You may even have strange dreams or nightmares. Pay attention to these. Consider writing down some of the dreams in your Grief Journal, too.

The important thing about despair is to let all feelings flow, no matter how weird they seem. Don't judge yourself. If you are crying all day, then go ahead and cry. Letting tears flow is good for you, believe it or not.

And if, for whatever reason, you have *no* tears, don't feel like a freak, either. Who says crying equals sadness? Grieve in your own way.

Let my hidden weeping arise and blossom.

— Rainer Maria Rilke

Try This:

COLLAGE

Sometimes we listen to music to let out our despair. Other times we read books or look at movies or television. Visual and audio images can trigger tears and let us express what feels like inexpressible sadness.

Take your Grief Journal out for a nonwriting exercise. Go through old magazines, ripping out pictures and words that appeal to you. Go with your gut reactions; don't think about it too much.

Now, paste those images onto two (or more) pages in your journal. See what pictures end up glued next to one another.

What words were you drawn to?

What colors do you see on the page?

There is no right or wrong way to do this exercise. It is simply about observing your gut feelings.

I am a rock.
I am an island. . . .
And an island never cries.

— from "I Am a Rock" by Paul Simon

Rage

If you are never angry, then you are unborn.

— African proverb

There is a moment when repression and depression turn to anger. Can you feel anger welling up inside of you?

You lash out at a teacher. You scream at your friend. You get mad at the bus driver. Anger is a sneaky thing. All of a sudden you're mad as hell — and you're not going to take it anymore.

Someone died? No way! He committed suicide? What a jerk! I got left all alone? I am so mad I could just — *aaaaaaaaaaaaaaaaaaargh!*

When you're this angry (and you may feel this angry at some point), you'll do anything to be heard. You may accuse people around you of contributing to the death. You may blame yourself angrily. You may vent directly to the dead person. *How could you leave me?*

By the way: Don't forget that a dead person *can't* hear you, so he or she might be the best target for rage, as strange as that sounds.

Don't Do It
Ashlee, age 15, Pennsylvania

BJ, I miss you so much. You've only been gone a short time, but it seems like forever. We had such big plans for the summer, fishing, painting your room, everything. . . . Now you are gone and there is nothing I can do about it. Nothing. I am sorry about our

71

fight. I told you repeatedly not to huff gas. Why didn't you ever listen to me? I miss you with all my heart. Maybe you died for a purpose, to show others that huffing is wrong, that children, teenagers, and anyone can die from it? Do you know that you are the first person to die from huffing in our county? Well, you are. I guess you got the stupid fifteen minutes of fame you always wanted. . . .

I went to your funeral. I stayed with you all day. It was so sad. Mom was so upset. I couldn't tell her enough that I loved her and I was here for her now. You knew huffing was dangerous, why did you do it? I would do anything to bring you back, anything at all. But you are gone. You aren't coming back.

I wish I could tell you I am sorry for being such a brat last week. I didn't mean for it to end like this. Mom sends her love and so do Dad and T.

I hope you are happy where you are. I know you will be. Did you get my ring and necklace? I gave you a purple heart. I have the same one, too. I want you to keep yours and meet me at the gates when it is my time. BJ, you were only sixteen. You had so much to live for. Huffing fumes is so wrong. Huffing is fatal forever. I don't want to see this happen to anyone else.

I don't mean to preach. I am sorry.

Yours forever, Ashlee

Ugly truths can be hard to face when it comes to anger about death. For example, how do you handle ambivalence? What do you do with your feelings if you didn't like the person who died?

Some other anger issues that arise in counseling:

- Just because people die doesn't instantly make them more noble or special. At first we may be inclined to think about that person in ideal terms. Over time, as you continue to embrace your feelings and reactions, you will find that your version of reality will emerge.

- You may feel abandoned. Here you are, all alone and angry, with no one to get angry at. You might get mad at someone who died unexpectedly, even when it wasn't his or her fault.

- What happens if you get angry at someone who didn't want to die? If you knew a person was doing everything in his or her power to get well and to be strong, and *still* died, how could you deal with that?

A powerful way to work through anger is to apply *negative* energy to a vital, *positive* cause that directly confronts the source of your rage.

If your friend died in a drunk-driving car crash, you might confront anger by wearing seat belts or volunteering with MADD (Mothers Against Drunk Driving).

If a cousin committed suicide, maybe you can start a teen chat room on the Web (or your own Internet support group) or volunteer at a suicide hotline to learn more about that subject.

Anger is like a thorn in the heart.

— Yiddish proverb

Notice or anticipate places where rage creeps up on you unexpectedly. Beat your anger to the punch by asking yourself provocative questions about how you really feel.

Are you suddenly envious of families that are intact . . . when you have lost your mother?

Do you resent groups of friends who are *not* directly affected by a classmate's untimely death . . . while you grieve?

Is your anger directed at the dead person? Are you mad at him or her for leaving you?

If feelings of anger are so monstrous that you cannot access them, perhaps what is needed is a simple solution. Try simply saying aloud, "I am angry," and see what happens. You may be very surprised at what tumbles out of your mouth. Or you may have nothing to say at all.

Remember: Try not to fight your anger. Grief is a process. Don't worry if some people run away because *they* are unable to cope with rage. Don't worry if you feel like a train wreck. Come face-to-face with the truth about your grief.

ANGER MANAGEMENT

You've thrown the killer tantrum to beat all tantrums. During football practice, you feel like body-slamming everyone. You are just so upset — and no one can help you! Try to manage your anger.

Of course you want to let out your real feelings, but the last thing you want to do is to alienate or hurt people around you. While grieving, you need the support of people in the months to come. Help yourself by expressing anger in safe, constructive ways.

1.   Punch a pillow or sofa cushion.

2.   Run around the block.

3.   Kick a rock to the curb.

4.   Join a sports team.

5.   Get out there and dance.

6.   Go to the gym and sweat.

7.   Bang a drum set.

8.   Have a pillow fight.

9.   Get a towel and strangle *that*.

10. Put on your car stereo, roll up the windows, and scream.

Chapter 6
Your Body

I won't hide you in my hands.
You can't live in my eyes, my ears, my voice
My belly, or in my heart. . . .

— from "I Give You Back" by Joy Harjo

Physical Changes

Just when your emotions are spinning in different directions, your body has boarded a roller coaster all its own. Do any of these physical symptoms look familiar?

- Appetite change
- Slow reflexes
- Rashes
- Itching
- Always tired
- Forgetfulness
- Breathing problems
- Colds and sniffles
- Headaches
- Clumsiness

- Nausea
- Weakness
- Abdominal pain
- Not showering
- Muscle tension
- Cramps
- Heart racing
- Overall sensory awareness
- Peacefulness or calm
- Back pain

Many times, focus is put onto the emotional experience of grief, but the physical aspects can hit you just as hard, especially as a teen. Your experience of the body is essential at this time. Growth and hormones are changing the way you look, the way you move, the way you eat and sleep, and more.

As grief starts, you're dealing with two bodies, that of the dead person being taken from you and your own. After someone dies, you may experience a deep sense of physical loss. Knowing that there will be no more hugs from the person who has died can leave you feeling empty inside. You will no longer *see* a person walking, talking, and laughing. Yes, we tell ourselves, the spirit lives on, but without seeing the body, we may feel lost.

Ironically, loss of another person might shift your focus onto your own body in an overly negative way. You might overeat. You might starve yourself. You might not sleep. You might run around a track until you collapse. You might take a sudden interest in indiscriminate sex. Side effects of the grieving process can affect not only your feeling emotions, but your feeling body. For most people, extreme responses are the exception and not the rule. As you grieve you are trying to get basic control over your behavior, but grief is not about becoming a controlling person.

Extreme responses help no one. You want to take simple steps.

Look for behavior connections that are *physical*. Pay attention to your attitudes about sex, drugs, or alcohol. If you find yourself using or overusing any of these, talk with someone. Try not to push yourself away from the reality of your body. Don't get so consumed by what you do and do not eat that you end up with an eating disorder.

Grief is about feeling the good, the bad, *and* the ugly stuff, however big or small. But it's not about sedating ourselves. It's about feeling all we can.

BODY PARTS

Where do you feel grief in your body? Write about it.

In your Grief Journal, jot down some of the physical feelings you have about death and grief. What do you feel around each of these body parts?

Ears	Eyes	Stomach	Hands	Shoulders
Feet	Chest	Mouth	Throat	Spine

The cure for grief is motion.

— Elbert Hubbard

When you feel grief in your limbs, in your stomach, and in your heart, try to get moving. Take steps to get your body out of the house, out into the fresh air, whether it's summer or winter. Go walk in the rain! Recognize how your body is behaving as you do this.

Do something physical for thirty to forty minutes a few times a week and watch things change. A lot can happen when you walk, jog, bike, swim, or Rollerblade. Maybe you can even go out for the hockey team or join the cheerleading squad. Do something physical for thirty to forty minutes a few times a week and watch things change. When the body exercises, endorphins are released. These natural chemicals inside our body make us feel much better. Believe it or not, exercise can keep us from having bad moods.

> *In a field*
> *I am the absence*
> *of field.*
> *This is*
> *always the case.*
> *Wherever I am*
> *I am what is missing.*
>
> *When I walk*
> *I part the air*
> *and always*
> *the air moves in*
> *to fill the spaces*
> *where my body's been.*
>
> *We all have reasons*
> *for moving.*
> *I move*
> *to keep things whole.*
>
> — "Keeping Things Whole"
>   by Mark Strand

In addition to moving around, try to eat right. Don't feel bad about eating an entire container of ice cream or a jelly donut once in a while. This is not a diet plan. It's an eating-awareness plan. Watching what you eat, having something from the salad bar at school, grabbing a piece of fruit, all of these simple actions give you an excuse to pay attention to *you*. Don't zone out. Your body needs you.

Drinking a lot of water is another essential body-related responsibility. It cleans out your system and eliminates toxins. People who are mourning often have increased thirst (from the stress, crying, talking to others, and so on). You probably don't want to be drinking diet soda all day long. Try to make a smarter choice by drinking water to keep your system hydrated.

Exercise, balanced eating, and drinking water are three positive things you can do for yourself. Right now, paying attention to your own needs is essential to moving through your grief.

It does not matter how slowly you go, so long
as you do not stop.

— Confucius

Food and the Body

Many cultures celebrate grief and mourning and reconnect with their bodies and spirits through food. It's a way to keep everyone, including the dear departed one, fed and connected in the midst of grief. In many cases, eating symbolizes the regeneration of life. We need to stay nourished to live, after all. Some cultures even believe the dead should take food with them on their journey to the next world.

What significance does food have in your experience of grief so far? As with everything else in grief, try not to stuff it away. Let it be a positive, nourishing thing for you.

The Meal of Condolence (Judaism)

After a death, Jews host a meal of condolence, also called *Seudat Havra'ah* in Hebrew. Jewish law says that the first meal after the burial of a loved one must be provided by friends. A typical menu may include lentils, hard-boiled eggs, and bread. All of these foods are associated with life in Judaism. During grief, Jews eat hard-boiled eggs to affirm hope in the face of death. The egg is particularly symbolic because it hardens as it cooks. A hard-boiled egg symbolizes a mourner's determination and ability to rebound from tragedy.

Saluting the Tomb (China and Taiwan)

During springtime in parts of Asia, families visit and sweep the tombs of their ancestors. Graves are often covered in peeled eggs, since eggs symbolize life. Other foods that are traditionally served on this day are three kinds of "grave cakes:" *hung kuei* cakes, *fa* cakes, and *shu chu* cakes. In Taiwan, *hung kuei* cakes are the most popular kind, with an outer layer of rice dough that has been dyed red and imprinted with molds that often show a tortoise, which represents long life. The food is an offering to the gods as well as a celebration of those who have died.

El Día de los Muertos (Mexico)

On the Day of the Dead, Mexican mourners prepare a picnic basket with a loved one's favorite foods, including loaves of bread in special shapes. Everyone joins in a procession to the cemetery to eat, sing songs, and reminisce about the dead person. At the same time, children play with wooden skeletons and skulls made of sugar with the name of the departed on them. After midnight, families and friends wait for the spirits of loved ones to visit their homes. An altar is prepared with candles, incense, photos, drawings, and — of course — favorite foods. Places are set at the table for dead loved ones, and special pumpkin bread and bread of the dead (*pan de muertos*) is cooked. A popular Mexican joke about this event describes two people visiting a cemetery together on the Day of the Dead. One puts flowers by a grave and the other puts food. "When is your dead one going to come up to eat the food?" asks the first person. "When yours comes up to smell the flowers," replies the second.

Nine Nights (Jamaica)

The Jamaican community supports the relatives of a dead person by helping to prepare a body's safe journey to the next part of life. Their special nine-night ceremony is held on a veranda or in a bamboo-and-coconut tent next to a house. Fried fish, cake, and breads sit on one table until midnight so that the spirit of the dead can drop by for a snack. Other parts of the ceremony include dancing, extensive singing, and lots of rum drinking. This is a party. Nine nights after the death, the ceremony ends. Journey cakes (johnnycakes) are also placed with corpses, accompanied by obeah or voodoo ceremonies that help put souls to rest.

The Doctor Is In

Don't underestimate the power of something as simple as food to help you heal in the grief process. You can also use food to share and comfort. Eating right is a way for you to take care of your physical self. Having a food "feast" is a unique way to remember the loved one who has died.

We held a memorial service for my daughter a year after her death. It wasn't a meal you'd order in a four-star restaurant, but it was perfect. Our menu included her favorite foods while she was alive.

- Mike'n'Ike candies

- Pizza

- Kirby cucumbers with "orange" dressing

- Tomatoes

- Roast chicken

- Five-color Lifesavers

You could have a feast for the person who has died in your life.

Put the deceased's favorite food and drink on your menu, and play his or her favorite music during dinnertime. You can even have people at the feast read poems and verse that your loved one would have enjoyed and appreciated.

What new memories can you make over a meal? You are bringing people together to grieve a sad loss but also to celebrate a life. For me, having a special menu in honor of my daughter fed and filled not only my body but also my heart and soul. Maybe it's time for you to feed your soul.

When you come right down to it, all you have is yourself. The sun is a thousand rays in your belly.

— Pablo Picasso

III
Situations

*There's no limit to how complicated
things can get, on account of one thing always
leading to another.*

— E. B. White

*A*ny kind of death is an abrupt interruption in your life. Different circumstances can make that death even more complicated and hard to bear. Due to the situation of death, your grief may last longer than you would like it to. Your responses may feel more dramatic than you are prepared to handle.

Whether death happens close to home or a million miles away, it can have an equally devastating effect.

Even if the situations are beyond your control, however, you have the ability to make things better after the fact.

Chapter 7
Death in Your "Family"

*Life is ten percent what happens to us and ninety
percent how we deal with it.
Life is like a fan. One day it blows, the other day
it sucks!
Life is like an onion. You peel it off one layer at a
time, and sometimes you weep.*

— Common wisdom

Traditionally, we define *family* as your primary care-
giver(s). This might be Mom, Dad, Grandma, stepparents,
brother or sister, foster parent, adoptive parent, or anyone
else who falls into that category.

Of course, family has a much larger context, too, especially in today's world. It includes your siblings, your closest
friends, your teachers (whom you see each and every day),
and even your pets. You probably have a school-year family,
a camp family, or even a neighborhood family. You surround
yourself with people who make you feel full inside.

When there is a death in any part of these families, you
will be impacted. Losing someone from your immediate family might affect you in long-lasting, specific ways. You've lost
someone you turned to in daily life for advice, someone with
whom you shared holidays and special events, and someone
who has watched and waited with you, maybe since you were
small. Losing that person can leave you feeling frozen. You
may feel unable to move on without that person.

Of course, you will.

TREASURE THE LIVING

Think about the things you know about your family unit. Preserve those memories on the pages of your Grief Journal.

Make a list of things good and bad you learned from the person who died. How did that person help you become the person you are?

In the wake of family loss, you may begin to treasure the living members of your family in a new way. *Carpe diem*, or, seize the day! Why not use some pages in your journal to make a list of why family is important to you.

Make notes about some of the promises you hope to keep to your surviving family members. Will you spend more time together now? Will you talk more openly? Will you begin to speak up and tell your family how you feel?

Even if you never do any of these things, writing them down is an important step in understanding your reactions and responses to this loss.

Losing a Parent

Why Did You Leave
Jolene, Age 17

You were so young, Mom,
And in good health,
Until the night of May 27
When you died of a heart attack.

We were so close;
We would always be there for each other,
You promised you would never leave me.
Now I feel so lost without you around,
I fall to the ground and cry and cry —
That's all I know how to do.
God, Mom I need you
More than ever right now,
But I know that you're gone physically.
You'll always be here —
You're in my heart, my memories,
And always remember I love you, Mom.

When we lose a parent or parent figure, our perspective shifts dramatically. What happens to your routines, your grades, and the rest of your life now that a protective figure has died? Who will cook dinner now? Sometimes we worry about things that seem so small compared to the "big" notions of life and death. This is natural.

What do you do if a parent dies and you're forced to move in with another relative? Or worse, what if you have to go live with another parent — the one you *don't* like? Losing a parent can mean losing a friend and losing the security of your living situation, too.

Dealing with the loss of a parent requires sober patience, especially for teens. The loss of a key family figure in your life may make the future look a whole lot scarier. Who will take you to the prom? Who will go shopping with you for that job interview outfit? Who will support you? Who will pay for college?

Perhaps the most difficult part of losing your mother or father is the loss of your own childhood. For a teen, the death of a parent means a lot more than grief. It means you must grow up *now*.

Losing a Grandparent

My Grandfather Bill
Lori, age 13, Pennsylvania

People said that he never frowned
But I knew he was bound,
When my dad told me he was going to die
I just wanted to cry,
During the funeral I knew he would be
Just sitting there looking down at me,
When they gave me the rose, I froze . . .
No one should forget him
I don't think they will,
'Cause he was just
The perfect Bill.

Because your grandparents are older, you may figure that their deaths may be more likely to occur during your lifetime. But losing a grandparent can come swiftly and take you by surprise. And losing the matriarch or patriarch of your extended family unit is like losing a part of your own identity.

When a grandparent dies, you may suddenly become aware of getting older. Now you look at Mom or Dad as much older, too. You have a heightened awareness of how quickly life is passing.

There are many emotional issues that come up after the death of a grandparent. How are you supposed to cope with your parents' vulnerability? The loss of *their* parents may mean you see them cry for the first time. Even though you are a teenager, you may find yourself acting more like your Mom or Dad's parent as you and others around you grieve the loss of Grandmother or Grandfather.

The Doctor Is In

Family dynamics can complicate your grief in a big way.

Death in the family may disrupt the ebb and flow of daily life. Sometimes it brings people close together, but it can also tear people apart. When the whole family gets into it, other issues besides grief arise. People revert to old patterns of knowing and handling things and let established conflicts intensify. You hope your family can rise to the occasion and deal with it, but they may not.

A big part of family grief involves not only grieving the deceased, but also adjusting to the new, minus-one-member family situation. Family members mourn Mom, but they also mourn the way the family used to be.

Losing a Brother or Sister

En Memoria Mi Carnalito
Valerie, age 18, Oregon

*Just sitting here remembering the times we used to
    share,*
*No matter all the fights we had I'm glad I knew
    you cared.*
*You always tried to stop the pain from breaking all
    our hearts,*
*A mamma's boy, a lady's man, you've been there
    from the start.*
*Now Almighty God has led the way, he's guided
    all your steps,*

He's taken you to a better place, he only takes the
    best.
And even though we miss you, baby, we know
    you're happy there.
No one can hurt your little heart, an angel unique
    and rare.
I promise I'll meet you there someday, the
    question's when,
For now I'll just try living on remembering back
    then.
One day we'll be together again and no one will
    feel pain,
So excited when I reach you my happiness will
    rain.
Don't know what to do without you, left us all
    behind,
The only man who loved me true and stood the
    whole damn time.
You were always the man of the house, a daddy
    and a brother,
Just struggling to hold us together: brothers,
    sisters, and our mother.
I want you to know you did succeed, no one to
    thank but you,
At times when I thought we wouldn't make it,
    those times you pulled us through.
Your little hands so strong yet young that always
    helped us through
Can now rest peacefully in heaven like they
    deserve to do.
Now you're in the Lord's sweet hands with happi-
    ness so pure,
It comforts me to know this now, too much you
    did endure.
Now you are returning home, to heaven where

you belong,
Where no one can ever hurt you again, no one can
do you wrong.
I love you, baby brother, more than my words can
say,
Every day I think of you and every night I pray.
I know that you rest peacefully, your little soul to
sleep,
And even though you've left us all, you're the
Lord's son to keep.

Sibling grief has its own unique conflicts. If you lose a sister or brother, you could become an instant only child. With one sibling gone, your family mood will undoubtedly shift. Think about it like a scene around the dinner table. Everyone reacts differently in small and large families. With one less person at the table, what do you think would change?

Brothers and sisters who once bonded together might argue now.

Unknown to anyone, the sibling who died may have been serving the role of buffer among the other siblings.

Or on the flip side, what if a sibling dies in a family filled with sibling rivalry? Grief may deliver guilt on cue. Surviving siblings will almost always have survivor guilt. If one twin lives while another twin dies, such guilt can be oppressive.

What do you reply if someone asks if you have any brothers or sisters *after* your sibling has died? Is the answer yes or no? Sometimes teens want to say yes and express love for the sibling who is gone. But there are many times when a sibling would rather *not* talk about the deceased.

Sibling death affects you in all areas of your life. You may suddenly have an awareness of your own mortality. When someone close in age to you dies, you're reminded that it could have been you. You feel terribly sad, but at the same time you may feel a deep sense of relief that your sibling died and not you. That is natural and okay.

Sibling survivors may also feel forgotten by parents in the middle of the grieving process. Forgetting is commonplace in families. It starts when Mom and Dad leave someone (you!) out of the funeral-planning process. They think they're doing it to protect you, but they're leaving you with the impression that you're not important enough to participate. What do you do when family friends send sympathy cards to your parents only? Doesn't anyone see that *you're* suffering, too? Why do you think people forget to offer condolences to the brothers and sisters in a family that is mourning?

Try This:

THE FORGOTTEN GRIEVER

Are you a forgotten griever?

Think about the events that have happened during the past few weeks. Have you felt forgotten, abandoned, or ignored? How? When?

Try not to feel self-conscious about these feelings. Don't judge yourself.

List at least five ways that you feel left out of the grieving process, whether by your parents or someone else.

What might you say to your parents to let them know how you really feel?

What can they do to help your grieving process?

Losing a Friend

I Wave Good-bye
Joe, age 18, Florida

You were once here by my side
Now you're gone and I wave good-bye
We were friends when we were small
We were friends when we grew tall
When times were rough we tried to work it out
We gave each other advice when we were in doubt
We always had fun together
Our friendship felt like it would last forever
Till the day came when your life must end
I said good-bye to my best of friends
I never thought that this would happen
My best of friends is now in heaven

Losing a brother or sister is tragic, yet losing someone from your extended family, like a close friend or a person you are dating, can be just as devastating. Sometimes it feels even worse than losing a biological sibling.

Why is it so hard?

After someone's death, you are forced to tear down all your dreams about that person. You may have fantasized about going on a trip around the world with your girlfriend or getting married to your childhood boyfriend. Now you see that you won't date or marry him, and having no future with that person really hurts. They are the ones who died, but they killed some of your ideas and dreams in the process.

That hurts.

In some cases, boyfriends or girlfriends may have to be mourned in secret. If you are in a homosexual relationship and your partner isn't out to his or her family, you cannot grieve openly for your loss. Once again, you suffer the initial loss, and then you get sucker punched by other complicated circumstances.

That's hard.

The death of a dear friend can mean losing your greatest confidant. How can you possibly find another person to tell all your secrets to? Who will you call when you need a shoulder to lean on? How will you show up at school on Monday without this person?

You will find a way.

Some people come into our lives,
leave footprints on our hearts, and we are
never the same.

— Unknown

Losing a Pet

Many who have spent a lifetime in love can
tell you less of love than a child whose dog
died yesterday.

— Thornton Wilder

Of course, there are family members we cannot forget: the four-legged, furry, scaly creatures in our lives.

How do we mourn family pets?

Therapists say people can learn a great deal about death and dying through pet loss. Do you remember flushing a goldfish down the toilet? Did your cat ever get hit by a car? Have you ever had an animal put to sleep? Pet loss may be your first intense memory of family death.

> CB's arthritis had gotten so bad he could no longer manage stairs and had trouble sitting down. My family had him put to sleep on a lonely Wednesday afternoon, after a good-bye photo session on the beach. I couldn't stop hugging him. We watched as they gave him a shot to slow his heart, and then he stopped breathing. We watched as the life left him, and I threw myself on his body and wept. His little pink tongue rolled out of his mouth, and the vet closed his eyelids so I didn't have to see the glassy stare. CB was dead. My attachment to that dog lived in such a deep, personal part of me. He loved me so unconditionally, like no person ever had. I walked, scratched, and fed him, and he followed me and wagged his tail to say "I love you." How could I go on without my beloved dog? Friends teased me about my love for CB. Of course I've heard the argument, "It's just a pet," but that is far from the truth. That pet's death was my first experience of grief.

— Laura Dower

Grieving a pet follows the same basic principles as mourning people. When you lose a pet, there's a great temptation to get a new pet immediately. You may want to fill the void left by the previous one. Try not to rush into anything. Find yourself a new kitty or lizard when you know you are ready for a new companion.

The way to Cat Heaven is a field of sweet grass
where crickets and butterflies play.
A cat may be late in getting to Heaven . . .
there's so much fun on the way!
But an angel will wait
at the yellow front door,
wait till a kitty
comes home.
And when she arrives,
he'll give her a kiss
and some milk
in a bowl all her own.

— from *Cat Heaven* by Cynthia Rylant

Chapter 8

When It's Complicated

Why is life so tragic; so like a little strip
of pavement over an abyss? I look down;
I feel giddy; I wonder how I am ever to walk
to the end.

— Virginia Woolf

Although we have no steadfast rules about how to grieve in everyday life, there can be serious complications, depending on factors like the cause of death. For example, how do you deal with suicide? What happens if you are the one who discovered the body?

Grieving can be an even more difficult process under extreme circumstances. When the situation is complicated, that may be a time to seek counseling or the advice of a therapist to help you move through your grief.

Make sure that as you grieve, you take into consideration how dramatic situations may cause you to feel more overwhelmed or cause you to react more erratically.

Violent or Sudden Death

Typically, your level of numbness can increase in relationship to how you learn about or witness a person who has died. You feel somewhat stunned *hearing* (from a relative, a friend, or even a stranger) about someone's death; but you feel utterly devastated to actually *witness* a death.

Of course, the circumstance of murder may be the most complicated kind of death. A homicide brings into play numerous other factors, like how could someone have done this, or how do I seek revenge.

After surviving a loved one's violent death, you may find yourself hit pretty hard physically: getting sick with the flu, getting headaches, or wanting to sleep a lot. You may feel especially traumatized by the death if your relationship to the deceased was an intimate one, like with a parent or girlfriend.

When a traumatic kind of death ends a vital relationship for you, your stress response gets way overcharged. Your body and mind are on the defensive, prepared to fight, freeze, or run away because this traumatic event cannot be undone. You may continue to relive the death in powerful detail, which causes you to structure your life to avoid whatever will remind you of that person or that trauma. You may suffer "post-traumatic stress disorder" (PTSD). Some of PTSD's common symptoms are recurring nightmares or flashbacks, insomnia, memory loss, difficulty concentrating, feelings of alienation, depression, phobias, changes in personality, and substance abuse. Do any of these seem familiar?

Chances are that even if you don't physically witness the event, the amount of detail you retain about the manner, moment, and aftermath of any violent death, even heard secondhand, can vastly affect your grieving.

If you are struggling and feel unable to get any moment of death out of your head, ask a therapist to help you explore your feelings right away. He or she can help with all your emotions, reactions, and overall health. He or she will also help you to see the death from an alternate perspective and to create distance between yourself and the event. Right now, part of what is so difficult for you is being so close to something hurtful that you can't understand or explain.

Finally, consider participating in a support group for other survivors of violent deaths, including both children and adults. Sometimes it helps to talk with others who have experienced painful and extreme circumstances like murder. Even though everyone's situation is unique, it helps to have someone who knows in some small way "what you're going through." There are people out there who *do* know. Check out the resources at the back of the book and in the chapter on Helping.

Try This:

CREATE AN OBITUARY

In the midst of extreme circumstances, take time to compose a thoughtful obituary of the person who has died. Sometimes when the pain of a death is too hard to bear, it helps to place our focus elsewhere, like onto positive accomplishments. Place your focus on the talents and pastimes of the deceased. This is your opportunity to reflect on all the wonderful things you know.

Open your Grief Journal to a blank page.

Jot down ideas about the kind of obituary you would compose for this person who has died. Do you remember the deceased person's favorite quote, place to visit, or song? Can you recall an anecdote starring the deceased? How many details do you want to include?

Write as much as you can for at least a half hour. When you're done, try reading the piece aloud in the person's memory.

Long-term Illness

Danielle, age 13, Illinois

I always wonder what my brother would be like now — if he would be tall, short, cute, funny, etc. I look at his picture and wonder what life would be like if he was still alive. I miss him so much.

My brother was feeling horrible, really sick, so my mom brought him to the hospital. My dad was on a business trip during this time so my mom told him not to fly back, that it wasn't that big of a deal. The doctors got the tests back and said it had something to do with his liver; they weren't sure. So they told my mom and my brother to go to a hospital in Chicago the next morning . . .

The nurse got ahold of my dad and told him to get back as soon as possible. The doctors got the tests back and they all went into a little room. The doctors told them that Kyle, my brother, had cancer. The doctor told them that this type of cancer was the incurable type of cancer. They would try their hardest but it was a 50/50 chance . . .

My brother went through chemo, blood transfusions, surgery, shots, and other stuff. I knew God was helping my family through this horrible year and I knew he was going to make it better. Kyle finally got out of the hospital after months of junk. He was like the other 3-year-old boys, getting into trouble but still he was kind and cute . . .

Then Kyle started to feel bad again and have pains . . .

The doctors talked to my parents and they had choices to get surgery in different states and chemo

*and other choices. But my parents chose to let Kyle
go. We went to Florida for a last family trip together,
it was so much fun to see a smile on Kyle's face! . . .*

*We got back and Kyle got really sick. He just
laid on the couch. On November 18, my little
brother Kyle passed away.*

I love him dearly and will forever.

Death from AIDS or other long-term illnesses like cancer
involve complications all their own. In many cases, we may
find ourselves living with a person who has contracted a disease that causes pain, crippling sickness, or slow deterioration. Because of this long process, we live with the idea of
death for a long time before it actually happens. This affects
our grief process in many ways.

When we bear witness to dying, we may have the chance
to prepare ourselves for death. We may even have time to say
our good-byes. But just because you know what's coming
doesn't mean it won't feel unexpected. Just because you
anticipate death doesn't mean it will sting any less.

Suicide

Sometimes we do not have a chance to prepare for death
and say our good-byes. Very little you do can prepare you for
dealing with suicide. There are too many factors involved.

You may be searching for a reason why the suicide happened.

You may be reeling from the shock and suddenness of the
loss.

You may blame a suicide victim for making a mistake.

Like any complicated situation, suicide has grieving rules

all its own. The grief guidelines in this book will help you begin to grieve, but you may need more specialized assistance in coping. Unlike death from disease or accidents, where we can point to a cause or a reason for dying that was beyond our control, suicide can be within a person's control.

I Am a Survivor
Leslie, age 12, Texas

I am a survivor, I will survive.
I wonder deep inside myself why I let him go.
I hear my sobbing, it shakes the heaven up above.
I see the world through shattered glass.
I want to be alone.
I am a survivor, I will survive.
I pretend he is still here.
I feel the pain seeping through my body.
I stroke the diamond teardrops that rest upon my
*   face.*
I weep for myself, I weep for him.
I am a survivor, I will survive.
I understand my tears and nothing else.
I say I'll be all right; I lie.
I dream of happier days, if only they would come.
I try to understand why I was left alone.
I hope he is happy now but I will never know.
I am a survivor, I will survive.

Note from Leslie: *I wrote, "I Am a Survivor" when I was eleven, three years after my father's suicide. Now, four years older, I hope that this poem might touch your hearts and deliver a message of hope. Grief has many stages. At that* time, I was still struggling with my father's death and was feeling increasingly uncomfortable with myself. The poem reflects that although I had undergone a devastating and life-changing experience, I was a survivor. The poem I would write today would reflect the hope and joy I have found through successfully moving through the grief process.

Did someone say that there would be an end,
An end, oh, an end, to love and mourning?
What has once been so interwoven cannot be raveled,
    nor the gift ungiven.
Now the dead move through all of us still
    glowing . . .
We who find shelter in the warmth within . . .

— from "All Souls" by May Sarton

Chapter 9
Stranger Mourning

Gift from Above
Laura, age 16, Minnesota

I saw my friends as they cried for you
But there was nothing for them I could do
I watched their pain and it hurt me so
When they had to let you go
Your time here was too short but important just
*   the same*
Your life we lost but your love was gained.
Their sorrow was great and your death was a
*   shock*
There was no room for smiles, no happiness, no
*   talk*
I didn't know you and I never will
But in my heart there's a place you fill
The impressions you left are too great to ignore
You shared your love and your heart will now soar
A smile you had for a friend or foe
But it's to heaven now that you must go
Watch over us please as we go on
To remember the memories that remain so strong
Heal our pain and remove our fears
To carry on your spirit and save our tears
This is to you with lots of love
From a friend of a friend you were a gift from
*   above.*

Strangers are people we don't know — although we may know *of* them. But those strangers can take us by surprise with the way they manage to rock our worlds after they die. The deaths of powerful figures, politicians, and movie stars sometimes lead to public mourning. Recently, this phenomenon seems to be on the rise. With cable TV, TiVo, the Internet, and other instant, in-your-face news outlets, it's hard to get away from the impact of the media circus surrounding a death. Memorial services and sobbing mourners are broadcast into your living room time and again.

Many of you may have already experienced this phenomenon of "stranger mourning." You may ask yourself if you are struggling with real issues of loss or are just following the crowd. Why are you sad about the death of someone you didn't even know? If you feel like you are mourning in any way, try not to question it. Any kind of loss can always feel real to you, even something you see on TV or read in the newspapers.

Princess Di's car wreck, the suicide of Kurt Cobain, and the disappearance and deaths of John F. Kennedy, Jr., his wife, Carolyn Bessette, and her sister Lauren Bessette were all showcased in around-the-clock news coverage. We responded emotionally and grieved for these young superstars. We got caught up in their dramas. We grieved — and we didn't even know them! It didn't matter. What impacted us was an emotional response to grieving in general. In their tragedies, we allowed ourselves to feel.

School shootings in Arkansas, Oregon, Colorado, and elsewhere have focused us on the deaths and dramas of children and teens nationwide. The phenomenon of "stranger mourning" for teens seemed to come to a peak with the Columbine tragedy in 1999. Children and adults of all ages were thrust into a grieving situation on live television. A year later, we revisited the tragedy and mourned all over again.

The events at Columbine had tremendous impact on the community. Students constructed an oversized memorial to victims, featuring balloons, cards, flowers, notes, and more. Kids took their grief LIVE! with their friends, their community, and TV viewers. E-mails and petitions on behalf of the Columbine victims were passed around on the Internet. Grief moved from a private experience into the public arena.

No More Tears
Nichole, age 15, Illinois

Only a small soul,
Can change the world.
Only a hurt person,
Can hurt so many more.
Only a ruined heart,
Can ruin so many lives.
Only a misunderstood mind,
Can go so far.

When I think of those two kids,
I have no more tears.
When I think of what has happened,
I have many fears.
When I think of the hurt,
I have so much pain.
When I think of the incident,
I wonder, "Will it happen again?"

So many gone,
Such young lives.
So much happened,
How could they live in those lies?
So much emotion,

Floating around in there.
So much pain,
Can't get it out of my hair.
So much senselessness,
How many times are we gonna go through it?
So much hate,
They just got up and blew it.

Why did they go
And cause all this pain?
We have no more tears,
They'll never do it again.

Note: This poem was written for the victims of the Columbine shootings, "for all the hurt . . . in Colorado — hoping that my pen pal is still alive," and distributed by e-mail.

If a common disaster hits close to home, we may want to relate to the situation, even if we know no one on the scene personally. Don't be alarmed by this. "Stranger mourning" connects us to people we would never know otherwise, people who seemed out of reach. Now we get to know them. That may feel important to you.

You also may have a strong desire to form a connection or bond with the sea of emotions at the scene. You want to be angry, sad, and open, all at the same time. At times, mass media mourning seems to rise above race, religion, and gender. It's about emotion and the expression of emotion. It is natural to want to feel deeply and to be a part of that. For example, Columbine became an outlet for teens to feel sad and get mad.

When you see strangers die, it may recycle a grief experience from your past into your present. Different losses stay connected to trigger responses in you, without your thinking about it.

Just as a seemingly mundane event like seeing a dead plant or losing a goldfish might trigger memories and emotions connected to a deeper loss from your past, watching someone die on TV, far away from your daily life, can also trigger old grief patterns and connections. Experiencing the public mourning of famous stars or tragedies in the news can make it happen, too.

The death of Princess Diana caused an international wave of grief — *instantly*. We'd seen her photograph staring at us from magazines and news reports for years, so she was a familiar stranger. Due to the media frenzy, maybe you felt like you knew her and loved her. The scenes outside both Buckingham and Kensington Palaces after Di's death spoke volumes: People from all over the world built a memorial to the Princess, leaving more than 10,000 flowers and cards and toys near their gates. We tuned in and watched her funeral. We mourned via the media and then went out to buy Elton John's tribute single, "Candle in the Wind." We felt a strong need to be a part of the mourning.

Grief was triggered when we least expected it.

Another thing to keep in mind when it comes to stranger mourning is that sometimes you may be mourning *more* than the loss you think you are. Grief happening right now may actually be deeply connected to other grief and loss from last night, last week, or last year.

These are just a few of mourning's many surprises.

If I am not for myself, who will be for me?
If I am not for others, who am I for?
And if not now, when?

— from the Talmud

United in Grief

No one needs a good reason to grieve, but Columbine became a compelling force of unity. It came on strong and the public got swept away. Sometimes it was all about the drama and less about the quiet places inside where people mourn. But remember this: Grief is *always* up to the individual. So if a person wants to grieve for someone he or she didn't know . . . so what? Isn't it good for that person to let those feelings go? Isn't it permissible for *you* to let those feelings go, too?

"Stranger mourning" doesn't corrupt grief, it takes it to a different level. We may have understood the possibility of mourning and feeling grief after watching entertainment on TV, but now we are regularly experiencing the emotional roller coaster of real-life situations that are miles, even continents, away. It makes us think about our emotions more. It brings up new questions, for sure. There are issues of privacy, for example. But more than anything, "stranger mourning" brings grief out of the shadows and into the spotlight.

GRIEF IN THE MEDIA

Think about grief as it is portrayed in the media. Ask yourself questions and jot down thoughts about this subject in your Grief Journal, or tear out newspaper clippings on stories about the deaths of strangers.

- Is it right or wrong, in our world of cell phones, beepers, laptops, and satellites, to be invading every private moment and turning every accident of grief into an event? How has technology changed grief for you personally?

- How would you feel if something like Columbine happened at your school? How would you grieve on CNN?

- How is technology helping to bring us to a more emotional place by allowing us to feel the pain of others on live television or by showing it to us on the cover of *People* magazine?

- Is it a blessing that "stranger mourning" connects us all in the great experience of life and now death, or is it a curse?

- As a teen who is faced with grief of your own, does this kind of "stranger mourning" affect you at all?

- Does seeing others grieve on TV make you feel like you have a shared experience with others, or does it leave you feeling even more isolated by your grief?

IV

Moving Through

In three words I can sum up everything I've learned about life: it goes on.

—Robert Frost

You set the pace at which you move through grief, but there is one primary destination. You are moving through to get back to *you*. No matter how significantly a death impacts you, there will always be some personal change happening inside of you during the grieving process. It just happens. You can't help it.

No matter how things change, however, you will *always* need to find your way back to a routine. You will need to get back in touch with your faith, and you will need to start the very difficult process of letting go once and for all.

Moving through is life going on.

Are you ready?

Chapter 10

Find Your Routine

Listen, children:
Your father is dead.
From his old coats
I'll make you little jackets;
I'll make you little trousers
From his old pants.
There'll be in his pockets
Things he used to put there,
Keys and pennies
Covered with tobacco;
Dan shall have the pennies
To save in his bank;
Anne shall have the keys
To make a pretty noise with.
Life must go on,
And the dead be forgotten;
Life must go on,
Though good men die;
Anne, eat your breakfast;
Dan, take your medicine;
Life must go on;
I forget just why.

— "Lament" by Edna St. Vincent Millay

Do you remember *why* life must go on?

Immediately following someone's death, ordinary life may come to a screeching halt. You attend funerals and memorial services. You stop doing homework. You don't go on-line

115

that much. You don't wake up on time. You're not paying attention.

After someone dies, day-to-day routines may seem a little pointless. Who wants to sit through trigonometry class or drama rehearsal? Who wants to listen to your friend complain about having no date for the prom? Who wants to write a ten-page paper on Jane Austen?

Since the person died, you may have changed patterns, adjusted rules, and shifted your schedule. You've strayed from your own routine.

Now it's time to think about getting it back.

Each day comes bearing its own gifts.
Untie the ribbons.

— Ruth Ann Schabacker

It may not be easy. You may feel like a part of you has been lost forever. Many cultures include a return to routine as a part of the time-to-grieve process. In Judaism, the passage of time is marked with the seven-day period of shivah. Everyone is excused from normal life to send condolences and say prayers. But when shivah ends, life's routine is meant to return to the way it was before the person died.

Your daily routine may be greatly affected by someone's death because you retreat from people and situations you used to enjoy and momentarily exclude people from your life. Now it's time to be with them again. People are essential to your grief because they are living, breathing, and full of information. Try not to leave them out of your life!

Getting in the Way

My hands don't hold you and my eyes
miss you . . . I go on looking for you, digging
you, dissolving you.

— from "No" by José Luis Hidalgo

Different things could be sabotaging your life's routine right now. During grief, you may let unhealthy habits get in the way of healthy ones.

Watch out for drinking and drugs. Do you suddenly feel reckless or angry? Examine new behaviors that have crept into your life since a person's death. Don't freak out if you've slipped into the out-of-control zone. You *can* get control again. Find someone to help you talk about what's happened.

As hard as it may be not to, try not to compare your grief to someone else's. For example, you and your mother are both mourning the death of your grandfather. Mom is devastated initially, but she bounces back more quickly than you. (You're still working through your shock and denial.) Mom says, "Get your act together! Get back to normal." You don't even know what normal is. Don't worry. The fact that your recovery time is a little slower than hers doesn't mean a thing.

Go where the grief takes you.

HAPPY LISTS

As you move forward, restoring and rebuilding your routine, take grief breaks.

Make "happy lists" of the small things in your life that make your routine work better.

Puppies and kittens

The latest DVD rental

Talking on the phone with your best friend

The warm, toasty feeling of being suntanned

Watching cardinals at the bird feeder

Hitting a home run during the play-offs

Jelly sandals or platform sneakers

Getting a package in the mail

What little things about your routine make you happiest? Make your own list in your Grief Journal.

As you readjust to life after death, observe social behaviors. What kind of reality have you built around yourself these days? What are your prevailing emotions? What overwhelms you? Name it.

Returning to routine will put some of your grief feelings into perspective. Start to see your life with a new set of eyes. You no longer have to feel pinned down by grief. A network of friends can provide support and help you reestablish yourself from day to day. As you get going, you can continue to make your routine as comfortable as it was before.

One way to ensure that you reestablish routine behaviors is to find a friend to be your supportive telephone buddy. Ask someone familiar if he or she is available to be "on call" for you whenever the pain of grieving becomes especially intense. This person will be there to listen to you when and if times get really tough. This way, if grief suddenly strikes, all you need to do is reach for the telephone and share your feelings. Do whatever you can to kick your support system into gear.

Motivation is what gets you started. Habit is what keeps you going.

— Jim Ryuh

Reestablishing Your Habits

In all areas of your life, with all the people in your life, you should begin to return to some kind of habitual behavior. These habits can be a tremendous source of comfort after your loss.

Your family. Do you usually have a certain meal together? Eat it. Do you have a gathering place that's your place? Go there. Make a connection with family members right after the death.

Your friends. Where did you hang out after school? Whose locker was next to yours? Did you walk to school with anyone on a regular basis? Find the school friends who know where you sit, what you have in the cafeteria, and other habits.

Your boyfriend or girlfriend. How has your relationship been working out during grief? Are you still studying together? Have you been behaving differently toward each other? Has your relationship suddenly become more sexual than it was before someone died?

Teachers. Are you turning in your homework assignments on time? Are you participating in class? Are you quieter or more rowdy during class?

Pets. Have you taken the dog for a walk? When's the last time *you* fed the iguana?

Work. Are you showing up on time every day? When is the last time you finished an assignment?

Every tomorrow has two handles. We can take hold of it with the handle of anxiety or the handle of faith.

— Henry Ward Beecher

For JR Forever
Melody, age 17, Oregon

I am Superwoman
I wonder how I am gonna go on
I hear all the sirens
I see all the flashing lights
I want to be free
I am Superwoman
I pretend I am an angel
I feel the clouds
I touch a hand that's lifeless
I worry about when the time will come for me
I cry when I see his face
I am Superwoman
I understand the meaning between life and death
I say it doesn't hurt, but I am lying
I dream of his face
I try to reach for him, but he's too high
I hope I'll see him again
I am Superwoman

One word of caution: As you finally do get back to your routine, try not to make erratic changes. Learn to prioritize what's important so you can regain control of your own situation in your own way. Remember that moving through grief is not about *fixing* something. You don't want to be a teen overdoing it, especially under stress or sadness. Superwoman and Superman need not apply here.

AS TIME GOES BY

Open your Grief Journal and write times down the left side of the page, starting at 7:00 A.M. and going through 7:00 P.M.

Now, write down the tiniest details of your day.

Put *everything* down on the page, from brushing your teeth to wrapping up the recyclables at your house. Don't leave anything out. *This* is your newest routine.

What kinds of activities do you notice most? What's missing?

Chapter 11
Find Your Religion

There is a light in this world — a healing spirit
— more powerful than any darkness we may
encounter. We sometimes lose sight of this
force when there is suffering and too much
pain. Then suddenly, the spirit will emerge,
through the lives of ordinary people who hear
a call and answer in extraordinary ways.

— Mother Teresa

Is There a God?

When death happens and grief begins, one of the most common questions teens ask is, "Is there a God?"

Another common question teens ask is, "How could a God let this happen?"

Grief brings up strong opinions and questions about God and religion.

Sometimes
Valerie Gallo, age 13, Pennsylvania

Sometimes I feel like giving up,
I don't know what to do — who to turn to.
And then I realize God gives me hope and
He's here to pull me through this.

123

Sometimes I am in situations
Where I don't know what's right or wrong,
Like I'm being crushed and then
I realize God will lead me to what's right and
He's here to pull me through this.

Sometimes I'm scared to death
Of what might happen tonight
Or what's going to happen tomorrow.
And then I realize that God will protect me and
He's here to pull me through this.

Sometimes I wish I could be someone else
Or have a different life
And I wonder if things will ever get better
And then I realize
God is here to pull me through this.

Sometimes I stay up crying
Thinking of all the pain and suffering
Others around me are going through
And then I realize
God will pull me and others through this.

Sometimes I wish I could take all of the mistakes
I made and erase them as if they never happened
And then I realize
God forgives if I ask and
He will pull me through this.

Sometimes I feel that nobody cares
And that nobody loves me
And then I realize
God loves me and
He will pull me through this.

So whatever you go through,
Even the hardest things,
Just say, "God will pull me through this."
Because he will.
I guarantee it.

You may mourn by digging deep into your religious heritage and tradition. At this emotional time, you may decide to question or even reject your own faith. You may feel Godless. On the other hand, you may be counting on God as the only one in the universe who can get you through this.

Here we are, more than halfway through this book, and grief continues to offer more questions than answers. Who is God? Who am I? Where is this taking me?

If All Angels Had Wings
Kevin, age 17, Alabama

Lurking around in this old world,
Are problems we all must face.
There's tribulations to make your head whirl,
That trouble the human race.
It makes one wish that he could fly,
To seek shelter from all the pain.
Really, all one can do is try,
To keep from going insane.
However, in the midst of this troublesome state,
When you feel as though you can't cope,
It never fails and it's never late,
Angels shine brilliant rays of hope.
It sounds strange and even odd,
To believe in something you can't see.
Fact is, placed on this earth by God,

Are angels walking with you and me.
They're not always in white with blonde curls,
They choose to wear a clever disguise.
Some dress up as girls,
And some dress up as guys.
They always offer a helping hand,
When you're surrounded by massive commotion.
Like a meager grain of sand,
Tossed upon the ocean.
Even as angels, they don't all have wings,
Instead they're just like you and I.
But if all angels did have wings,
You could rise to your feet and fly.

Different cultures and religions all over the world have grieving and funerary rituals that identify what kind of role God, if God exists, can perform. Many people turn to their own religion to help guide them through these tough times. If you are a Christian, you may count on your church to support your grief. If you are a Jew, you might visit the temple. If you are a Muslim, you might pray at your mosque.

What About Heaven?

One of the most common questions that arises during the grief process is the desire to know what happened. Where did the deceased go?

Is there a hereafter, heaven, or great beyond?

As we all know, the answer to that question cannot be proven scientifically. You hold the answer in your heart. Some people think we are reincarnated, while others believe we return to the earth for good. Many Christians believe in heaven, hell, and purgatory — a sort of waiting room before the final destination. Individuals who have survived near-death experiences often tell of a white light we walk toward after death. The belief in supernatural beings such as ghosts and spirits offers the possibility that dead people still walk among us in a different form. Of course, there are also atheists who believe that there is no God and, therefore, no afterlife.

You're allowed to believe anything you want. Just as there is no *right* way to grieve, there is no single answer to the possibility of an afterlife. Human beings have spent centuries asking ourselves questions, performing experiments, searching our souls for the answers. Many people want to believe that the world beyond is even better than this one. In that world, we may even be reunited with those who have died before us.

Here on Earth

Sometimes the process of grief may be made better by taking control of what you can, and putting aside what you can't control. Just as with issues of guilt and regret, you can only change and adjust what lies ahead of you, not what lies behind. When it comes to religion and afterlife, you might want to focus on what you can prove and control, not on what you cannot.

Of course, if you believe in heaven, then believe in it fully. You may feel doubtful. Your emotions may tempt you to put aside your beliefs and opinions, but try the best you can to stay true to your belief system. These beliefs will help you to feel comforted by the notion that the person who has died has moved to a safe place. It may help make the separation easier to bear. Just as everyone grieves differently, everyone may also *believe* differently.

Listen to your heart.

*Blessed are they that mourn, for they shall be
comforted.*

— Matthew 5:4

God's Whisper
Megan, age 16, Texas

*God saw you reaching for the sky.
I prayed, "Dear God, please don't let Daddy die."
He whispered gently to him,
"Come on, it's your time to go,
Say good-bye to your dear family,
Tell them you love them so.
Wish them well, a happy life,
Don't let their souls break down and die.
Rest their broken hearts assure,
That you fought hard to the end but found no cure.
The tunnel light is getting bright.
The angels' songs will make you strong."*

MEDITATION

Sometimes quiet reflection can help you find yourself and your center again. Have you ever meditated before? Meditation is a way for you to collect your thoughts. Read through and then go back to do it. You need to close your eyes for the real thing.

Find as much silence as you can. Sit in any chair. Sit on the floor if you want. Now close your eyes, sitting very still. Test your senses.

What do you hear? Crickets, sirens, people talking.

What do you smell? Bread, bleach, your perfume.

What do you taste? Jelly, toothpaste, nothing.

What do you touch? The fuzzy carpet, your thigh.

What do you see? Nothing. Quiet. Peace.

Feel your eyes relax. Is religion *inside* of you?

Religion in Nature

It is possible that, for you, religion won't be found in the Bible or the Torah. Maybe in your grief you will look for evidence of God in other places. Sometimes becoming one with nature can help you become religious. Try to get outdoors.

Outside you may find God all around you, in the sun, the rocks, and the streams. You may find spiritual experiences almost anywhere you look — but you will need to look. A walk in the woods or listening to the wind, such simple moments can literally take our breath away. Suddenly, we feel enriched. We have the capacity to transcend our fears and face our fears about death and grief with renewed strength.

Every so often, when I look
At the dark sky, I know she remains
Among the old endless blue lightedness
Of stars; or finding myself out in a field,
In November, when a strange
Starry perhaps first snowfall blows
Down across the darkening air, lightly
I know she is there, where snow
Falls flakes down fragile softly
Falling until I can't see the world
Any longer, it's only stilled shapes.

— from "The Last Hiding Places
of Snow" by Galway Kinnell

When one door of happiness closes, another
opens; but often we look so long at the closed
door that we do not see the one which has
been opened for us.

— Helen Keller

Whether it's out of books, a holy ceremony, prayers, or deep in a forest, open yourself up and let religion come to you. It will come in an assortment of shapes, sizes, and colors.

Whether you decide you get religious power from a church, a mosque, a temple, or wicca, what matters is that your choice works for you. And if you choose to *not* believe in God, then that's fine, too. Find a person you can trust and speak to when you feel low and overwhelmed by the grief. Find someone to believe in who will believe in you.

Don't forget: You can act as tough and strong and self-sufficient as you want, but you may need some form of consolation and support even when you think or say you do not. Maybe it's church, maybe it's a friend, maybe it's meditation — or maybe it's just you, the trees, and your Grief Journal. Consider the possibilities.

Of course, be smart about these choices, too. You do not want a religion that promotes any kind of control over your thoughts or actions, as is the case with some organized "cults."

Be sure to let grief in — and then out — and let yourself grow in a healthy way.

Remember the here and now. Remember the person who has died as he or she *lived*. They're an essential part of your faith now. Perhaps you feel that person is watching over you. Continue to move through and live your own life in the present with his or her good influence and inspiration as your guide.

Good-bye; remember me as loving you.

— Toni Stone

Try This:

AFFIRMATIONS

A great way to connect with your positive spirit is to use positive affirmations. Words and thoughts are powerful things. An affirmation is a statement you make to yourself that emphasizes hope, possibility, and strength. Usually, the power of affirmations comes from repeating them. You affirm what you know about yourself and your ability to move through grief.

In addition to (or instead of) reading the Bible, the Koran, or another religious text, repeat affirmations aloud. Repeat each one at least twice. You can repeat them silently if you want to keep them private. Copy them in the margins or on the covers of your school notebooks. Scribble them on notes you tape to your bathroom mirror.

Affirmations echo the facts about who you are and how you are surviving this grief process. They *affirm* your desire to get through mourning. Use them creatively. Then make up some of your own!

My religion is very simple.
My religion is kindness.

— Dalai Lama

Affirmations for Grieving

- I will trust the process of grieving.
- I am open to all ways of resolving and dealing with my grief.
- I will let myself be happy.
- I welcome my own growing spirit.
- I welcome life.
- I see tomorrow.
- When I tell my story, I let it move me.
- I put my trust in the unknown because I have to.
- Laughter is the best medicine.
- I am grateful for my friends.
- Through grief I will learn something beautiful about the person who died.
- Through grief I will learn something beautiful about myself.
- I have strength.
- I have the ability to love.
- I have the ability to grow.
- I know how to share my strength and my sorrow.
- I have the power to understand my sorrow.
- I will be patient and grieve for as long as it takes.
- It is acceptable for me to take care of me.
- I don't have to take care of Mom and Dad 24/7.

- I do not need to pretend that I am stronger than I am.

- I look around me and see others who may need help with their grief, too.

- The dark cloud overhead will pass by me. I will be fine.

- I need someone to help me cry.

- I have the power to keep moving on in my life.

- I give myself credit for having the strength and courage to survive.

- Moving through grief, I have gained insights.

These are the days we live
As if death were nowhere
in the background; from joy
to joy to joy, from wing to wing,
from blossom to blossom to
impossible blossom, to sweet impossible blossom.

— from "From Blossoms" by Li-Young Lee

Chapter 12

Letting Go

*And the good-bye makes the journey
harder still.*

— Cat Stevens

So we grieve aboard an emotional roller coaster, we find our way back to some kind of routine, and ultimately we realize it is time to let go.

When exactly is grief supposed to end? For many people it won't ever stop completely, but it will let up. It will remain in one way or another, shifting and changing but in a more managable way. For some the process happens immediately, but for others it can take months.

One thing is certain. You need to make the first move. You need to relax and let go.

Try This:

RELAXATION

Sometimes it's hard to let go because you are holding emotions and tension in your body. Are you having trouble falling asleep? Are you feeling clumsy? Believe it or not, these can be connected to how you grieve.

At bedtime, try this simple visualization to relax your mind. Create a mental image of a warm, tropical place. The waves are gently lapping the shore around you. There is a soft, warm breeze on your skin. Stay in that place. Take a few deep breaths and really *see* and *hear* the water.

If you are taken aback by sudden anxiety and worry at home or school, you may need to relax your whole body. Imagine sitting in a large, open field. Overhead, the sun has found you and sends down its warm rays. Feel them enter your body, flowing from the top of your head into your chest, your arms, your hands, your stomach, your hips, your thighs, your knees, your feet and toes. The light is making its path through your body so you can get rid of the dark spaces where the grief hurts. Feel how warm the sun is.

Do you feel your body relaxing? Meditations and relaxation exercises can be a great way to help yourself fall asleep, too. Letting your physical self go is as important as letting go of your fear, rage, and doubts.

Kate, age 17, Minnesota

Dear Jim,

It's been eight months since I said good-bye to you. Eight months can bring a lot of change, but I still miss you. I hate that person who killed you. I hate that they took you away from everyone who cared.

I remember sitting under the big old trees in my front yard and lying in the soft Kentucky bluegrass, watching the clouds. We never really did do much, it was all talk of plans and things that concerned us. Needless to say, you cared for me. I know that now.

You made sure that everything went right with everyone around you, and that's how you got into trouble. You wanted to see the strain of good in everyone, but you were just too blind to see bad this time. I miss you. Every day is a barrage of memories of my last day seeing you alive. What happened to that smile? Why did it have to go? I feel bad for still having my smile.

I want to ask if you will help me now. I understand that this is your vacation of sorts, but I really need you. I want you to help me through this so I can understand. Put the words that make sense to me. I wish you were here for a minute just so I could hug you and tell you that you mean something to me. I hope that where you are now is a good place and you are happy.

I miss you. Please wait for me. I'll be coming someday.

The Doctor Is In

When you let go, you release the pain and the relationship with that person as you knew him or her on Earth.

But you do not let go of emotions, memory, or the impact of that person.

The part of the grief process that allows us to let go is the same part that guides us ahead. As you let go, you want to say good-bye in your own way.

Naming what the person who died meant to you emotionally, physically, spiritually, or *any* way is a powerful act. It can be a part of letting go of who they were and moving forward with what you can now hold on to of them.

Near, far, wherever you are,
I believe that the heart does go on.

— from "My Heart Will Go On,"
love theme from the movie *Titanic*;
music by James Horner and lyrics by William Jennings

What is the formal definition of "going on"? What are the signs of letting go?

I know I am getting better and stronger when . . .

- I can be alone at home even though the person who died is no longer there.

- Memories of the person who died make me smile, not cry.

- I laugh at my friends' stupid jokes.

- I make stupid jokes.

- I can concentrate on doing homework or writing a paper.

- I can drive around without feeling sadness for the person who died.

- I can get out of bed in the morning without feeling like lead.

- I am no longer tempted to skip classes or skip school altogether.

- I can listen to the radio without hearing songs that make me cry.

- I am beginning to make new relationships again.

- I am looking forward to holidays.

- I am beginning to make more plans for weekends and vacations.

- I start inviting friends over to my family's house again.

- I start flirting, dating, or attending school functions again.

- I no longer avoid the telephone or the doorbell.

- I am turning the energy I spent grieving into energy spent doing things I love to do, like playing on a sports team, joining an after-school club, or just hanging out.

- I'm getting my hair cut, buying a new outfit, or getting a makeover — and taking care of me again.

- I feel good about my physical appearance again.

- I no longer need alcohol or drugs to make me feel worthwhile or to dull my pain.

- I no longer need a physical relationship to make me feel loved because I accept myself.

- I sleep well every night and wake up refreshed each morning.

- I have regular eating habits. I am no longer starving myself or eating in secret.

- I can talk about the person I lost without getting upset.

- I survive momentary grief lapses, when sadness or anger overwhelms me. I make it through to the other side with a keener sense of awareness.

Rachael, age 16, Kansas

Dear Steven,

Every night before I go to sleep, I whisper how much I love you. I always thank you for spending what little time you were here on earth with me and for giving me the best feelings of my life. I also tell you that no matter what happens, I love you the best, and we are soul mates and we'll be together one day. I don't really need to tell you all of this again in a letter; I don't need to tell you what happened to me today like I always do. I'll tell you tonight that you are with me somehow. I have all of our feelings and experiences.

When I found out that you were very sick, I got this ball of desperate hope and intense love and fear in my stomach. On the night of May 4, that feeling only disappeared into sadness and dread. I felt you leave and was waiting to hear from your family that you had died. I know it would sound funny to others, but I know that we are connected somehow, despite the distance of miles. Finally, I got the confirming letter from your mother, confirming your death, and I felt like this depressed sadness came rushing at me and literally hit my body.

The raw pain I was experiencing was way too much for my body to bear. Your family and friends were halfway across the country and did not know me all too well and I had no one to turn to. My friends meant well but couldn't understand.

This pain is still as strong as it was before, then, but now I am able to get on with my life. I know you want me to be happy. Thank you for that. I will grow up, get married, and have children, but you will always be in my heart. And I know that as my soul mate we will meet again.

Thank you so much for making me feel the way you did. I know that we are absolutely perfect for each other. You brought out the best in me, and I am a better person because of you, thanks to you. Everyone loves you, and I know you are a good and loyal friend and watch over all of us. You loved me more than life itself, and I returned your love the same way. I could feel you crying, "I love you, Rachael, I love you," before you died, and I responded, "I love you, Steven, I love you, baby."

It didn't surprise me when your best friend told me in a letter that you had cried that out to me over and over. I can never again with anyone on this earth feel the love and bond that I felt and still feel right now with you. I won't feel that way again in this lifetime. But I know that I will feel it again when I see you.

You are my star and my guardian angel. Thank you.

LETTERS TO HEAVEN

As you let go, write a letter, a poem, or an e-mail to heaven. At this point in the grief process, what would you like to say to the person who has died?

Do you want to thank him or her again?

Do you want to take a walk down memory lane?

Do you want to reassure the person that you'll be seeing him or her again?

Do you need your communication with the dead person to be in the form of a monologue or a dialogue?

While doing this exercise, painful emotions may return, may get caught in your throat perhaps, or inside your belly.

Think back to the chapters on guilt and regret.

Remember that this exercise is difficult, but that it's a task borne in your feelings and imagination only. It is what you make it. You are the one in control of your feelings and responses.

Now, take out your Grief Journal and write your letter.

Don't forget that it doesn't have to be all words, either. Doodle or scribble. Make it into a paper airplane. Put a note in a bottle and send it into the sea.

Mourning Isn't Always Sad

Count the night by stars, not shadows.
Count your life by smiles, not tears.

— Proverb

As you have seen in the Grief Journal exercises throughout the book, writing about your feelings of grief, happiness, anger, and other experiences can be enlightening. But don't forget that the journal is a place for you to let go in more ways than one. You do not have to be "serious" to mourn. Let your playful side get a little exercise right now, too, and watch what happens.

The Doctor Is In

Remember that even in the midst of the most powerful grief, you may discover the finest medicine of all: laughter. Don't *ever* feel bad about laughing. You won't always express emotion on the dark side. Some of it will be more upbeat. It's okay to laugh during and after you have grieved.

Laughter = life.

Here are three different exercises you can do to get in touch with the gladness that can be found under the surface even during the most troubling grief. It is natural to want to feel happiness with your sadness. They go hand in hand. You should not be bothered if you have an impulse to laugh or giggle, even if it's at a funeral. Just try to keep in mind that when you do have an impulse to laugh at a serious time, not everyone around you may understand why. Explain it to them. It's another chance to open up a dialogue about feelings and grief. Laughter can even keep you healthier. It can function as a natural analgesic, which means that it raises your body's threshold for pain and relaxes your muscles, too.

Snaps

Get an instant camera and take a roll of pictures. Try to do it all in one afternoon. These can (and should) be photos of anything and everything. If you want to, take a snap of someone's knees, or snap the passing clouds, or even snap yourself holding the camera out in front of you.

This is not an exercise in photographic excellence. This is about capturing what you see while you're grieving and exploring how you react and respond. When the photos are developed (try to do that within a week), sit down with them. What do you see? What reminds you of the person who has died?

You can also pull out old photos of the person who has died and ask yourself the same questions. What do you remember seeing and feeling on the day when the photo was taken? How does that memory help or hurt right now?

Name Poem

Many of the poems in this book are serious examinations of circumstances and loss surrounding a person's death. What if you wrote a poem that was more silly than serious?

Take the letters in the name of the person who has died, writing one per line as you go down a page. Think of words

beginning with each letter, and write a line across that speaks
to a funny memory of that person. For example:

J oked all the time, liked to rhyme
O pened his eyes wide when he laughed
E veryone loved to be in his company

Dream Theme

Sometimes it's hard to write a poem or a story without a specific theme.

You can get ideas for themes everywhere. Open any book or magazine, point with your eyes closed, and see where your finger lands. Got an idea yet?

Sometimes when we feel choked by feelings, it helps to write or talk or even think about something else. What you may find is that "something else" will lead to a better understanding of your grief. A theme poem just may uncork some feeling or memory you've been keeping bottled up inside, helping you to let go.

Here are some themes to consider. Make up your own, too.

- Hope
- Butterflies
- Friendship
- Sports
- The future
- A wishing well

- Water
- Sunlight
- Faith
- Bravery
- Nature
- Flowers

*The main thing in one's own private world is
to try to laugh as much as you cry.*

— Maya Angelou

V
Remembering

That which was bitter to endure may be sweet to remember.

— Proverb

*L*etting go does not mean you are forgetting. It means you are making room to remember. Remembering is central to all grief.

As you remember, you fill in the places where loss took place. You make music out of the silence. You pour light into the darkness.

Think about memories as colored beads. We take each one and string them together like a necklace. They are like pieces of jewelry, or keepsakes, that you can bring out whenever you want them or need them.

Chapter 13

I Will Remember You

Katie
Jessica, age 13, Pennsylvania

The one who had the best smile.
The one who had the best jumps.
The one whom everybody admired.
The one who had a lot of confidence.
The one who got her back handspring.
The one whom everybody loved.
The one who loved cheerleading.
The one who helped us to win.
The one who had a lot of personality.
The one who had the red hair.
The one who had the freckles.
The one who made us all laugh.
The one who always wore her Adidas.
The one who always blamed things on J.
The one who we always kicked in the butt.
The one who always put K. up.
The one who had the best facial expressions.
The one whose hair would never curl.
The one who always had a guy to talk about.
The one who fought for her rights.
The one who got an H in English.
The one who had makeup but did not know how
*   to put it on.*
The one who threw a pencil at the UPS guy and
*   got trash duty.*

The one who always had a smile on her face.
The one who will always have a space in all of our
    hearts.
We love you, Katie.
You are the one.

For a few months after someone dies, there is a close focus on survivors. You have survived the shock, denial, fear, anger, and relief up to this point. You have moved *through* grief, just as you wanted to do. But there is still work to be done.

There is still the *most* important work to be done: remembering.

"I will remember *you*."

Look for the details of a life lived by someone you cared about, while remaining mindful of the fact that the death is still new. You are still raw around the edges when it comes to reliving moments from your joint past. Tread lightly as you go.

Try This:

ALL IN THE DETAILS

Think about *everything* small that you can remember.

Take your Grief Journal to a quiet place that reminds you of the person who has died. Now write. Describe the deceased. It is all in the details.

Rather than remembering big actions or lasting legacies, look at the *smaller* characteristics.

What kind of shoes did he or she wear?

How did she or he usually dress?

What did his hair smell like?

What did she wear in the wintertime? Summertime?

What did his or her voice sound like?

When did you first meet?

What was the first thing he or she ever said to you?

Instead of weeping when a tragedy
occurs in a songbird's life,
It sings away its grief.
I believe we could well follow the pattern
of our feathered friends.

— Robert S. Walker

As you work through your arsenal of emotions and grief responses, you may remember things that were not positive. It could also be that remembering feels way too painful right now. Take your time letting memories back into your mind, heart, and life. Just as all grieving experiences are unique, the act of remembering varies from person to person, too. Just because someone is unable to remember the deceased does not mean he or she mourns that person less.

A Letter to My Dad
Meggy, age 16, California

Dear Daddy,

Today they told me that the face I made at them looked just like the face you always used to make. It's been almost six years since you were killed, and I just can't remember. I can't remember what your voice sounded like or the words you said to me. I can't remember what we did together or what it felt like to hug and kiss you. . . .

We never got into the screaming fights all my friends had with their fathers — I wish we could have. You won't be able to give me away at my wedding or meet your grandchildren. They won't be able to understand you. I don't know if I do.

I really hate the fact that I can barely remember what it was like to have a father, Daddy. But I know that you will always be with me. . . .

We like to think that the memory of a loved one will live forever in our thoughts and prayers, but there may be moments when remembering is hard. As time passes, you may begin to lose touch with some of the day-to-day information about the person who has died. You will feel like you don't know the person anymore.

Try not to get upset. You have worked and moved through grief to a place where remembering is like a second skin. You don't have to think about it so much anymore — it just is there. Trust what you know, deep inside. Trust what you feel.

The Doctor Is In

Do not worry if you seem unable to remember even things you were sure you knew about the person who died. It *is* in your mind. It *is* in your memory. And it *will* become available again.

Don't curse the darkness — light a candle.

— Chinese proverb

Remember me when I am gone away,
Gone far away into the silent land;
When you can no more hold me by the hand,
Nor I half turn to go yet turning stay.
Remember me when no more day by day
You tell me of our future that you plann'd:
Only remember me; you understand
It will be late to counsel then or pray.
Yet if you should forget me for a while
And afterwards remember, do not grieve:
For if the darkness and corruption leave
A vestige of the thoughts that once I had,
Better by far you should forget and smile
Than that you should remember and be sad.

— Christina Rossetti

Fifty Ways to Remember

Below is a list of fifty ways to help you as you remember and grieve.

You can consider the first one on the list in progress already, since you began your Grief Journal while reading this book.

1. Start a book, recording all the memories of your loved one that you can think of. It really helps to look back at it and read all about things that you remember. Have you started a Grief Journal? If not, consider starting one now.

2. Reminisce with friends about good times you shared with your loved one.

3. Put all your photos of the deceased in one place where you can look at them easily.

4. Save a copy of the memorial service flyer or photos. Laminate them for safekeeping.

5. Take two pieces of the dead person's favorite food and eat one piece for you and one for her or him.

6. Plant a special garden, and put a small statue, maybe an angel or fairy, in it.

7. Watch home videos of times you spent together.

8. Make personalized memorial cards for the dead person and his or her family.

9. Call the person's family on the anniversary of the death.

10. Create a memorial web page in honor of the dead person.

11. Wear an item of clothing that reminds you of the person who died.

12. Climb into the person's bed, and pull the covers over your head. Or, climb into your own bed and do the same.

13. Have a birthday party without the birthday boy but in honor of him.

14. Visit the family, listen, and make phone calls to them.

15. Get flowers or a plush toy that the person would have liked. Cuddle the toy.

16. Help make a display of meaningful objects for the funeral or memorial service. Or create a display on a tabletop at school or home.

17. Speak at the dead person's memorial.

18. *Always* refer to the deceased by name in conversation.

19. Write out your favorite memories of the deceased and give it to the family.

20. Invite other survivors to join you in activities honoring the dead in your community.

21. Share a book on grief like this one.

22. Write a poem about the person who died, and have it printed in the school paper in memory of the deceased.

23. Have your own ceremony of good-bye in which you write a note to the one you love and then release it in a balloon. Of course, make sure the balloons are friendly to the environment.

24. Light a candle at mealtime.

25. Burn incense.

26. Read the deceased person's favorite poem or short story aloud.

27. Make a mix tape with songs from the deceased person's list of favorites.

28. Put on perfume like the scent that the deceased person wore.

29. Put up a special photograph of you with the deceased.

30. Display a special object from the person's own collection or an object someone gave you.

31. Memorialize the deceased in a short prayer.

32. Wear a colored ribbon in honor of the person who has died and in honor of others, too.

33. Volunteer your time to a group or cause that was important to the deceased.

34. Volunteer at a hospice.

35. Make a memory collage from old photos and magazine clippings.

36. Make a shadow box with three-dimensional objects or art in memory of the person, and ask your school to hang it in the library.

37. Donate books in memory of your friend.

38. Plant a tree in the name of the person.

39. Wear jewelry or carry an object that belonged to the person.

40. Paint a picture and hang it in your school library in honor of a friend or teacher who has died. Have everyone sign his or her own message to the painting.

41. Set aside some quality time alone to meditate.

42. Spend an afternoon doing *exactly* what your friend or

family member used to like doing best (going to an art museum, bowling, etc.).

43. Read stories about losing a loved one. There is a reading list at the end of this book.

44. Talk to other mourners at an on-line chat, and share your memories in cyberspace.

45. Do something to help a stranger.

46. Do something to help your grandparents or parents.

47. Do something to help a teacher after class.

48. Visit the cemetery.

49. Clean your room and do other chores.

50. Use your hands instead of your head to remember! Sculpt a bowl or vase and paint it the favorite color of the deceased. Fill it with flowers regularly to remember how much you cared about that person.

Try This:

QUILTING

One of the most famous acts of mourning and remembering in the twentieth and twenty-first centuries has been the NAMES Project AIDS quilt. Since the early 1980s, families and friends have designed and contributed squares to an enormous quilt sewn in the memory of all those men, women, and children who died of AIDS. The quilt has traveled internationally to honor those lost to the disease and to raise money for families and individuals now fighting AIDS.

Have you ever made your own quilt? You can do this on your own or with friends. A quilt can be a wonderful way for a group of people to remember someone together.

Using fabric, colored paper, photographs, and other items, have mourners assemble individual squares (they should all be the same size; a six-inch square works well) that evoke a memory of the person who has died. Perhaps one square is all green, the deceased's favorite color; another may be a poem the deceased loved, written on fabric with a fabric marker. Be inventive. Brainstorm as a group the memories that seem most precious and most telling. When the squares have been finished, assemble them together in your own quilt. If you don't sew, paste or tape the square together.

I Simply Yearn
Missy, age 18, Pennsylvania

When I look back on the days of my youth, I recall many memories filled with smiles, laughs, and you. Along with your memory, I also recall many mixed feelings. When the guys weren't around, I was always "your little girl," but when they were, I was picked on and cried hysterically when I felt I didn't receive enough attention from you. Now, five years later, I desperately miss the way you showed your love for me, which was unique from any other love I knew. . . .

Now I yearn for the days when I swore I only came second to you — compared to the guys. I yearn for the moments when I always said, "Gramps, get with it!" I yearn to make you banana splits like I used to, I yearn to have your open arms

*cradled around me when I had a bad dream, and I
even yearn to play hairdresser with the little hair
you did have and parade you around the house,
having a fashion show.*

*You always expressed your love to me in a way
very different than any other way I knew before. I
now simply yearn for you.*

Flowers grow out of dark moments.

— Corita Kent

Sometimes remembering happens in a very public way, whether in a large scale memorial, or in living gardens.

After the Oklahoma City bombing in 1995, a memorial was erected in honor of the adults and children who died as a result of the explosion. A stone chair resembling a tombstone memorializes each person who died. Visitors can leave flowers or draw chalk messages near their loved one's chair. Elsewhere at the memorial a large pool is surrounded on either side by a giant gate. The one on the left says 9:01 A.M., while the gate on the right says 9:03 A.M. The reflecting pool in the center shows a time of 9:02 — the exact time of the explosion.

We can also memorialize with plants and flowers, perhaps even by planting a memorial garden. The gift of a living memory, the familiar colors and fragrances of a garden will give you comfort, year after year.

Planting trees can also memorialize someone. Oak trees represent strength. Willow trees represent releasing and making a new start. Cypress trees represent endings. Yew trees symbolize immortality.

Consider roses as another symbolic way to remember. They add scent and color to any memorial garden. Some roses have special names that can represent a special meaning. These include roses such as Cherish, Fragrant Cloud, Pink Peace, and White Dawn.

Seeing or reading about examples of larger-than-life or living memorials may inspire you to organize a community memorial of your own. Remembering and mourning together can be a cathartic community activity.

The Doctor Is In

One of the most important places you may need to remember is at school. Sometimes people around you, teachers, administrative staff will be too stunned to organize anything on their own. You can help them to organize a school memorial.

First, arrange with the teachers how the memorial will be planned. Is the whole school to be invited, or is it exclusive to your grade only? Work with your school to ensure that your plan is understood and accepted by the deceased's family.

Next, decide what you will do for the ceremony. Will you be reading poems? Can you play a song the deceased liked or perhaps played on the guitar? Can you light candles at school?

Decide if you want to put a plaque in the library in honor of your classmate. Or maybe you want to plant a tree on the school grounds.

Finalize who will be participating in the ceremony. Will the principal or superintendent of schools need to say a few words? Should you invite the person's family? Will other students get up to share their memories?

As a motivated student, you have the power to show that you care and that the rest of the school should care, too. In addition to a special memorial, you can also organize a Memory Circle, a small group of kids who meet to commemorate and share the loss together.

Start a Teen Grief Group

After someone in your school or neighborhood dies, you may want to create your own special teen group to talk and share grief experiences.

Remember that this group is not meant to be a therapy group, but rather a place where you can remember, mourn, and share — supporting one another. Your goal in forming the group is to let people know they are not alone in grief.

- Inform school guidance counselors, therapists, and youth leaders from your community. They can help you get set up. They can also suggest the best *place* to meet. Can you use a location at school or will you meet in your living room?

- Put up flyers at school, and advertise in newspapers and church bulletins or anywhere else you might find interested teens. See if you can advertise for free in the classified section of a local newspaper. Perhaps you can call your grief group "A Gathering in Memory of _____."

- When you have a list of participants, call people to invite them to their first meeting. Personal connections matter.

- Consider whether you will allow nonteens (your younger brother or someone's mother) to attend the group. If you do make the group exclusive to teens, then you need to consider a way to include others in the experience of the group. You don't want your group to seem like it's shutting people out. Maybe you can have one meeting to which *everyone* in your community is invited.

- Start your meeting by stressing a rule about confidentiality and privacy. You want your group to be a safe environment. Also, try to set a time limit — perhaps an hour — on the meeting and on future meetings. The goal is to forge a connection and reassure teens who may feel lost in their grief. Keep the meeting contained and supportive.

- Encourage everyone attending to share his or her personal story, but try not to pressure anyone to speak. Sometimes a person would rather be silent. Other times, people may choose to speak about topics unrelated to grief. Gently try to keep the meeting focused on memories and feelings about the person who has died.

- Don't be afraid to joke or laugh. There are no rules about how the meetings should happen. Not everything about remembering as a group needs to be serious.

- Plan things to do. You may want to serve refreshments, too. Maybe you gather to view a movie. Perhaps members of the group read poems or sing songs that mattered to the deceased.

- Decide as a group how long your meetings should continue. You will need to plan an end to the meetings, just as you need to take on some sense of closure for grief. Host a final party, barbecue, or other activity.

Days of Remembrance

Mourners around the world take time to remember those lost and loved. Our calendars designate days to celebrate religious tradition and also to grieve for those lost during wars and battles. What days of remembering are important in your life?

March 27	*Holocaust Remembrance Day*
Good Friday	*Remembering the Death of Jesus*
April 4	*Victims of Violence Day*
April 28	*National Day of Mourning*
May 15	*Peace Officers Memorial Day*
Last Monday in May	*Memorial Day*
August 6	*Hiroshima Day*
August 9	*Nagasaki Day*
August 15	*Kan-Ban (Buddhist Day of the Dead)*
Second Sunday in September	*National Pet Memorial Day*
October 31	*Celtic Feast of the Dead/Halloween*
November 2	*All Souls' Day/Day of the Dead*
November 11	*Canadian Remembrance Day*
December 1	*World AIDS Day*

*We have what we seek. It is there all the time,
and if we give it time, it will make itself
known to us.*

— Thomas Merton

Chapter 14

Aftershocks

Linus: After you've died, do you get to come back?
Charlie Brown: If they stamp your hand.

— from *Peanuts* by Charles Schulz

Once the grief process has ended, your life may resume its normal schedule. Well, as normal and crazed as teen life is. And then one day, out of the blue — it's back! Grief comes slinking back into your backpack, your locker, and your life. And coming right back with it are sadness, loneliness, and exhaustion. You may dread the thought of hopping aboard that emotional roller coaster again.

Try not to worry. You're experiencing what grief experts call aftershocks. These are little (or big) rumblings to remind you that you have a lot of feelings at your fingertips. An association, a photograph, or a word might all send the memory of the person and his or her death back to you. You are especially likely to be reminded of someone who died during the holiday season or around the person's birthday.

Aftershocks may take you by surprise, but they will come and go. This doesn't mean, by the way, that the grief work you did failed. *Everyone* has aftershocks. We can't help ourselves. What you need to do is mark on your calendar, in advance, times that may be more difficult and keep an eye open so you don't get slammed by guilt, fear, and a bunch of other stuff out of the blue.

Some of the most common times when you may feel an aftershock are listed here. How do these "special occasions" make *you* feel?

Pain is inevitable. Suffering is optional.

— Anonymous

The Anniversary

What do you do on the week/month/year anniversary of a person's death? Do you send his or her loved one a card? Do you hold a memorial service?

The answer to all of these questions is yes, or whatever else you feel like doing to celebrate the anniversary of the death, even if that means doing nothing at all. Remember that your memories will continue into the next year and the year after that. It seems impossible to face this date at first, but it will get easier over time. You will find ways to cope that work for you. You may need to hold a Remembering event on each anniversary. You may also choose to remember quietly. The choice is yours.

The Birthday

On your deceased family member's or friend's birthday, can you set up a remembrance spot in your home? Can you buy a birthday cake and celebrate the day in his or her absence? Can you sing "Happy Birthday" to someone who has died?

Yes. Yes. Yes.

Celebrating the birth of someone who has died is a special thing to do. In celebrating birth, you celebrate his or her life. What a brilliant thing!

Don't forget to make a birthday wish, too. Thank the person who has died for giving you the gift of himself or herself while alive.

Valentine's Day

A loved one left you with sentimental memories that make this holiday extra hard to bear. In fact, you feel like eating a pound of chocolate in three minutes! Valentine's Day can become unbearable.

Do you get irritated when you see flowers and candy being sent to friends? Are you upset by a TV show that has two characters getting romantic? Does this day make you feel like you will never love again, since your boyfriend or girlfriend has died?

Valentine's Day may be a hard holiday for anyone who isn't in love, let alone for someone whose loved one is deceased. Sometimes what makes it most difficult is that it is a holiday on which people give, send, and share objects of their affection. Here you are, sharing with no one.

But you have the power to change that.

In memory of your loved one, you can make this a *private* holiday. Spend time recognizing the love in your heart, and don't worry about receiving the flowers and candy — buy 'em for yourself! Rent a romantic video, and let yourself have a good cry. Or listen to a love song and do the same. It sounds sappy, but the old saying, "Better to have loved and lost than never to have loved at all," has meaning. Your heart hurts, so treat it like you would any wound: Dress it, comfort it, and make sure it gets *lots* of attention.

If you aren't so good at being alone, call up a good friend and ask him or her to share the day with you. Make the first move. Every holiday is what you make it. There are no right or wrong rules (no matter what the folks who write greeting cards say!).

Memorial Day

Sometimes any holiday that celebrates veterans or the memory of soldiers reminds us of those who have died in our own families and extended families. We attend Memorial Day parades and think about the people we have lost.

You can pick a quiet time to have your own private Memorial Day for any kind of memorial you wish.

The Box
Jessica, age 17, Minnesota

I was in the attic today
And I found a dusty old box.
I opened it up
And looked inside.
The memories started
To flood my mind,
Just as the tears
Flooded my eyes.
I found the picture album
With the pictures of us
Through the years,
The notes we wrote
Back and forth,
And some of the "junk"
We bought at the mall.
As I was looking
Through the box,
I realized I can hold
The pictures, notes, and junk,
But what I really want
Is you to hold.

Mother's Day/Father's Day

How are you supposed to deal with these holidays when Mom or Dad is not here? Is it hard to hear about other people's mothers and fathers on these days? Do you feel angry when you go into the greeting card store and see the Mother's and Father's Day cards?

Maybe you need to make a card of your own on this holiday to celebrate the memory of your lost parent or grandparent. You might also plant a tree in the name of your deceased mother or father, and then celebrate their memory as you watch the tree grow over time.

Mothers and fathers (that is, your parents) who have lost a child (your sibling) will also be mourning on these days. They're mourning because they don't want to be reminded about being a mother or father right now. You might make a card or draw a picture for parents feeling vulnerable or sensitive on these holidays. Remind them of the qualities that make them special.

Thanksgiving

You may say with anger, "Remind me again what I have to be thankful for?" Of course, that's exactly what needs to happen: You need to be reminded. Friends can help to get you talking about all the blessings in your life, including love for the deceased.

Think about the word *Thanksgiving*. It means a time to give thanks, as we know. But examine the word *giving*. How are you giving while you're here? Tell someone how you feel.

I took the last
dusty piece of china
out of the barrel.
It was your gravy boat,
with a hard, brown
drop of gravy still
on the porcelain lip.
I grieved for you then
as I never had before.

— from "What Came to Me" by Jane Kenyon

Christmas/Hanukkah/Passover/Easter

On religious holidays like Passover or Christmas, stay calm and experience the fullness of the tradition. Did you do something special on this holiday when the deceased was alive? Remember it publicly or silently.

You can purchase or plant flowers in honor of the deceased. Celebrate with a Passover or Easter feast. On Christmas, perhaps your family can light a candle in tribute to the deceased, or sing a carol or hymn dedicated to their memory.

On religious holidays, you can always recite a special prayer.

New Year's Eve

You might find it hard to see a year ahead when the last year was so rough. How can you think about new beginnings and resolutions when it seems like everything has ended?

Think about this: New Year's is a time to reflect on what has gone past, but it is also a time for a clean slate. As the refrain goes, "Sweep out the old, and ring in the new!" What better holiday than New Year's Eve to let go of the person who has died?

Sometimes your aftershock experience means that you will need to go back again and look at tougher stages of grieving. Review the chapter on Letting Go in this book. Sometimes a new year is a symbolic time for you to let go.

There are many other possible aftershocks. Any date that felt important before someone died may be even more important now. Being around other loved ones can trigger strong emotions, too. If your cousin dies and then you see your aunt, you may begin to feel grief for your cousin all over again, even years afterward. Other times to pay attention:

- The start of school

- Weddings

- Confirmations

- Bar mitzvahs or bat mitzvahs

- Family reunions

- Any kind of gathering that you may have attended with the deceased at school, camp, or home

In her book *You Can Heal Your Life*, Louise Hay explains, "If you want to clean a room thoroughly, you will pick up and examine everything in it. Some things you will look at with love, and you will dust them or polish them to give them new beauty. Some things will never serve you again, and it becomes time to let those things go." You may want to get rid of thoughts, beliefs, and attitudes that no longer serve you well. Try to move through grief's aftershocks in the same way you moved through your earliest grief experiences: carefully.

The Doctor Is In

Sometimes your aftershocks are like barriers reconstructing themselves all around you. You're not specifically grieving anymore, but you're as protective as ever of space, ideas, and emotions.

You're afraid to get close to someone in case he or she dies, too. You feel guilty for having a new close friend right after someone else has died. Your own actions may surprise you. Sometimes you grieve more at the *happy* times in your life.

After my daughter died, we prepared to cope with the anniversary by celebrating her with memorial services each year. This was a time during which our friends honored her memory, sang songs, and talked about her short life. Whatever you do, try to make a plan in anticipation of aftershocks. You may tell yourself you will rent a movie, take a journey, sleep over at a friend's house, or just sleep all day. Even if your plan is to do absolutely nothing, it is still a plan. You are preparing in your own way. Even the simplest plan can help you from becoming overwhelmed by grief's aftershocks.

SHOCKS

There are other kinds of emotional responses you need to watch out for. Try to keep a record of your own personal aftershocks inside your Grief Journal. Are any of these aftershocks familiar? How?

- Dreams, nightmares, and "visions"

- Anger and upset you may feel while visiting a cemetery or a memorial

- Returning to favorite places you went — with someone else

- Hearing songs on the radio or TV that remind you of the person

- Hearing someone talk about the person

- When someone calls your number by mistake, looking for the person

- Stumbling across an old photo album

- Holding or seeing something that reminds you of that person

- A particular time of day that could make you think of someone

In the midst of winter, I found there was within me an invincible summer.

— Albert Camus

VI
Helping

*So long as you can sweeten another's pain,
life is not in vain.*

— Helen Keller

*Y*ou may need to help someone else to get on with their grieving. Helping a person to grieve can teach you a lot about yourself, too. At this time in your life, you may try to get by without anyone else's interference or help. But part of the process here is learning that at times when you ask for advice, counsel, or assistance, you are not acting weak. The strongest people need help of all kinds.

In fact, no one can really survive grief without *some* kind of help from family, friends, or a counselor.

Knowing when to ask for help and when to offer help can make all the difference.

Chapter 15

When Someone Else Is Grieving

Unless someone like you cares a whole awful lot,
nothing is going to get better.
It's not.

— Dr. Seuss

As with so many things in this guide to grief, the most essential thing in helping yourself or someone else get through grief is to be aware. Just be there.

Listen. Let the person who is mourning talk about the loss. Let the grieving person talk about the loved one who has died. Sometimes silence says a lot more than your words can. People who are mourning need to tell their story as many times as you will let them. Sometimes the stories will be repeated. But each time the story is told, the finality of the death sinks in. A good listener needs to accept feelings of anger, frustration, disappointment, fear, and sadness. A listener needs to encourage the mourner not to keep anything bottled inside.

Do not feel you have to offer advice. As tempting as it may be, try not to spout your own grief wisdom. There is no need for you to take the responsibility for fixing the situation. Just bear witness to it. As you now know, no two experiences are the same. Let mourners own their grief experiences. Even if you have been through the same type of loss and have a similar approach to life, your advice may have the effect of making the grieving person feel angry, judged, and frustrated.

Touch. Another important way to help a grieving friend is to reach out and stroke that person's hand or offer him or her an embrace. Trust that the person will tell you if they are uncomfortable with the gesture. In many cases, touch also speaks louder than words.

Jessica, age 14, Georgia

Dear Melissa,
    Everyone would say "I understand," but I want to scream because they didn't lose their best friend. I wrote this to all those people who wouldn't stop saying they're sorry.

Please allow me to grieve.
Don't tell me that you understand.
Don't tell me that you know.
Don't tell me that I will survive.
How I will surely grow.

Don't tell me that this is a test,
That I am truly blessed,
That I am chosen for this task
Apart from all the rest.

Don't come to me with answers
That can only come from me.
Don't tell me that my grief will pass . . .
That I will soon be free.

Don't stand in pious judgment
Of the bonds I must untie.

Don't tell me how to suffer
And DON'T tell me how to cry.
My life is filled with selfishness,
My pain is all I see.
What I need is love, I need your love,
Unconditionally!

Accept me in my ups and downs,
I need someone to share.
Just hold my hand and let me cry
And say, "My friend, I care."

Do not free a camel of the burden of
his hump; you may be freeing him from
being a camel.

— G. K. Chesterson

What *Not* To Say: The Wrong Words

One of the most important ways you can help someone who is grieving is by being aware of what you *should not* say or do.

Avoid using clichés to help your friend. Do not make statements that are "closed," leaving no room for further discussion and exploration like, "Time heals all wounds." Better to tell a grieving child, teen, or adult something that invites that person to talk openly about their feelings.

Try not to rescue people from their guilt feelings, which are natural and normal during the grief process. Remember that each person grieves in his or her own way, and each must be allowed to grieve in his or her own time, too.

Be patient. As someone who wants to help a mourner, the worst thing you can possibly do is rush in to fix a situation. Of course, your intentions are well meant. You want to remove the griever from a sad place. But don't forget that moving through sadness and the other emotions is the only path to understanding the death that has occurred as well as the future that lies ahead. We endure the pain to see the rainbow on the other side. Each person must do this for himself or herself.

Below is a list of watchwords and phrases you may want to avoid saying to someone who is grieving. Try to imagine how the words you say will be heard. You can never know what another person is thinking or feeling. Let that person do the talking as often as you can.

Some of these expressions may seem harmless. But give them a second thought. As you read each one, notice the words in *italics*. These are possible responses to your statements. What do you think your responses would have been if someone had made any of these statements to you?

- I understand how you feel.
  Do you?

- You'll get over it.
  Do you want to tell me when?

- Your father/mother lived a full life.
  How do you define full?

- You must be strong.
  How do you define strong?

- It was the will of God.
  What if I'm not religious?

- Don't cry.
  Isn't crying a part of the process?

- You shouldn't get angry. Rage is a terrible thing.
  Isn't anger a part of the process?

- It's wrong to feel jealous.
  Isn't jealousy a part of the process?

- Be brave. Buck Up! Chin Up!
  What if I don't feel cheery or brave?

- (Name of deceased) is better off where she/he is now.
  Where is that? Were they worse off here?

- Move on — get on with your life.
  But wasn't that person a part of my life?

- At least (name of deceased) is no longer suffering.
  But what if I would rather have her suffering as long as she could be here and not gone?

- Just be patient.
  For how long?

- Don't you think you should be over the grief by now?
  Why are you telling me how I am supposed to grieve?

- You need to be active and get out more!
  What if I don't feel like it?

- You're young. Be thankful for that.
  What about the fact that being young means I have that many more years to live with the loss? What if the future looks even bleaker to me now?

- You'll find someone else to share life with/be with/play with.
  But what if I want to be with the person who died?

- Quit feeling sorry for yourself!

Would you want someone to say that to you?

- Why are you so upset that your brother died? You didn't even like him.
  What if that just makes grieving him harder? What if I still want to mourn someone I didn't necessarily like?

- You're doing such a wonderful job!
  Who said mourning was a performance and that I was supposed to be rated on mine?

- There must have been a reason.
  You know this is not necessarily true. I understand that life is not always fair or reasonable.

*Suggestions for People Dealing
with Bereaved Teens*
Hayley, age 14, Illinois, whose three-year-old
brother died in his sleep

Don't be afraid when I cry. It is healthy and normal to cry. If you don't know what to do when I cry, give me a big hug.

When I say I am okay, I am probably not. A loved one who meant a lot to me just died, and I am not okay with that. Please excuse me if I am rude or snappy. So much bad happened in such a small time. I am even having a hard time being patient with you.

Don't assume that I know you are upset about my loved one dying. Let me know by giving me a big hug.

When you get uncomfortable when I talk about my loved one, it makes me uncomfortable, too.

Don't think that talking about my loved one will make me upset. I want to talk about my loved one very much.

What to Say:
The Right Words

When you finally do have an opportunity to speak, you may rack your brain to think of the right words. General, simple words of comfort are always a safe bet. So are questions to get the mourner talking, thinking, and feeling comforted and cared for.

Asking easy questions is always a good thing.

Don't be afraid to say the dead person's name. Share specific memories, then invite the mourner to do the same.

- I am sorry for your pain.

- What was your relationship like?

- Can you tell me about the death?

- Is this painful for you?

- I am sorry. How can I help?

- How are you doing? How is the family doing?

- Were you close?

- I have no idea what it must be like for you; I've never had a (spouse/child/parent) die. Can you tell me what it's like?

- Is this hard to accept?

- I really miss (name of deceased). He (or she) was a special person. I miss (offer specific memories or a short story). Tell me what it's like for you.

- I'm here if you need to cry.

- I am here for you whenever you need me.

- I've never experienced this before, and I just don't know what to say to you.

Piglet sidled up to Pooh from behind.
"Pooh!" he whispered.
"Yes, Piglet?"
"Nothing," said Piglet, taking Pooh's paw. I
just wanted to be sure of you."

— A. A. Milne

Try to help someone who is grieving to face up to (and to *not* ignore) his or her own experience of grief.

Help them find safe and nurturing emotional outlets at this difficult time. Death and dealing with death can feel suffocating. Relationship conflicts with family members often occur. There are side effects to grief that someone trying to help can look for and be sensitive to. If you are helping someone to grieve, then give that person the space and freedom to feel. Above all else, never judge a grieving teen — or *anyone* who is grieving. Would you want someone to judge you?

Even though everyone grieves according to his or her own timetable, help a griever to move through guilt and regret and through *all* aspects of grief as painlessly as possible. Remember to watch for symptoms that signal when grieving may not be going very well. If you notice behavior that seems intense or unusual, then you may need to help that person by intervening or by getting him or her professional help.

Watch your own responses and reactions to a death. Let your responsible actions and feelings serve as the best advice and example. Sometimes adults don't want to talk about the death to teens or others, assuming that by doing so they can spare people pain and sadness. By not sharing your own grief, however, you can leave someone feeling more isolated in their grief. No matter how much you hide, people will grieve anyway, so go ahead and share what is *really* going on inside of you.

Confirm that it's all right to be sad and to feel a multitude of emotions when someone dies. Help the mourner to see that the hurt felt now won't last forever.

Be There for Me
Jennifer, age 16, Texas

Times have been rough and emotions unsteady,
Life turned upside down and many tears shed.
It is during these times that I need you.
I need you to hold my hand and walk with me
To listen to what I have to and yearn to say.
I need you to hug me and let me know that it is
*   okay to cry.*
To let me know that you won't leave me.
I want you to help me to ease the pain.
I want you to know me, how I feel and what I am
*   thinking.*
I need you to listen, not to say what you think is
*   right.*
For we all know that no words can ever heal the
*   pain,*
But the comforting touch, the feeling of knowing
*   that you'll be my friend,*
To listen, to hug, to hold.
I need you most when I seem like I need no one at
*   all.*

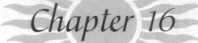

Chapter 16
Finding Professional Help

At all crucial moments in our lives, we want
to speak without knowing what to say.

— J. Coates

Sometimes you may need the guidance of a professional to get through grief. You have many options about how to ask for help, where to look, what to expect, and how to respond to it once you get it. Are you unsure about where and how to begin? That's a perfectly normal response.

Many teens have a whole list of reasons why seeing a professional may feel intimidating or overwhelming. Do any of these sound familiar to you?

- I can't afford a therapist. It's too expensive.

- I don't want anyone to know my business.

- They'll ask me questions I won't want to answer.

- People will think I'm crazy.

- Talking about the death will only make me think about it more and it will only depress me.

- They will tell others private things from my life.

- How can I trust a complete stranger?

- I don't have the time.

- I don't want my parents to know I'm having this much difficulty.

- I can just talk with my mom/boyfriend/sister if I need to.

- I'm fine. I just want to forget about it.

Take a deep breath and remember that asking for help is not like jumping off a cliff. You can always stop. You can always change your mind. Plus, you can get help with your family, too, with a group counselor. Getting help may feel scary, but it should always be safe for you. Explore your many choices before saying "no" or "yes" for sure.

There's *Still* a Dark Cloud Over Me

One of the most important things to do when considering professional help is to identify where your situation has gotten too difficult to manage on your own. Maybe you realize that it's been a while since your loved one died and you're still not bouncing back from the grief. Maybe you're very depressed. There are distinct signs that this could be happening to you.

- Appetite changes that have caused major weight gain or loss

- Upset sleep patterns that leave you unable to rest or have you sleeping excessively

- Long-term withdrawal from your peers or family

- Risk-taking behaviors where there were none before — like drug and alcohol abuse or sexual experimentation

- Inability to experience pleasure no matter what

- Feeling overwhelmed by anger, fear, or hopelessness

- Only feeling happy with drugs and alcohol

- Thoughts of ending your own life

How do you know if you *really* need extra help or if you should choose to stay home and deal with it alone? If you have *any* of the above symptoms, seriously consider a visit to a counselor or therapist — even if it's just one visit. When you can't shake the depression, you may need to talk about it or have someone examine it and give you a professional diagnosis.

Yes, this is scary. But you're a survivor, remember?

You can always walk away if you decide it isn't right for you.

So take the first step. Try it.

How about unabashedly bawling your eyes out?
How about not equating death with stopping?

— from "Thank U" by Alanis Morrisette

Is There a Doctor in the House?

As you begin a search for a therapist or other doctor to help you make it through the roughest patches of grief, give consideration to who that person is. This means looking at that therapist's credentials and beliefs and seeing how well the two of you fit together. Chances are that you may need to find someone who does not know you. You may feel like someone who knows you would have a hard time staying objective. Your therapist should have no hidden agenda.

You need to find a therapist who has a high threshold for unbearable emotion. This means looking for someone who is willing to talk about *everything* you need to explore. You do not want a therapist who tries to get you to conform to any emotional norms that don't feel right to you. As said over and over again in this book, defining what is normal is complicated, but your therapist's job is to help you find your unique path through the grief. Having a therapist doesn't always mean doing it *their* way. It means having one-on-one support as you do it *your* way.

Here are some things you need to ask yourself and to decide before selecting a therapist.

- Decide if you will feel more comfortable with a man or a woman.

- Make certain he or she is ready to protect your confidentiality. Of course, therapists do this, but when you are a teenager, it's *extra* important to know that what you express and say won't be shared with parents without your explicit consent. Naturally, if you are dealing with huge issues, your therapist may suggest that you do share things with Mom and Dad — but be clear about what that will be and when that might happen.

- Do you want a therapist or counselor who is old or young?

- Figure out what kind of counselor you can or cannot afford. What kind of medical coverage does your family have? Do you need to seek counseling from a more cost-effective resource, like a free community service organization, or can your therapist work on a sliding scale (ie. you pay what you can afford)?

- Does it matter to you whether the therapist has specific religious beliefs or is of a certain race? Sometimes you might feel like talking to someone who seems to be "like you," and other times you might want someone who has new ideas, fresh opinions, and who can offer you the kind of comfort and/or guidance you may be looking for and are not finding elsewhere.

- Does a therapist's training matter? Do you want to see someone with medical training (a psychiatrist) or non-medical training (a psychologist, social worker, and so forth)? Ask questions so you know what the differences may mean for you as you work with a person.

- Try to make a written list of questions before you visit any therapist or counselor. Be prepared to ask for what you want. Chances are that once you step into a stranger's office, your mind may wash blank or be abuzz with jumbled thoughts and emotions. Your list will come in handy at exactly those moments. Write it in a quiet place, over a period of time. Maybe you can keep it in your Grief Journal.

Support Groups

Another way to get help is to dive right in and ask for what you need in a group setting. Are you confused about your grief? Ongoing discussions with other people might help you.

Are you willing to acknowledge in a public forum how your feelings about death affect you, or would you rather discuss them one-on-one? If you decide to go with a group, look for one that specializes in teen issues. Hunt around for a group and a combination of people you like. You *can* shop around. Just because your parents like a group doesn't mean you will. Talk to them and find one that works for everyone involved.

When you move into a public forum with peers who are also mourning, it may not get better right away. A group dynamic might simplify or complicate the situation. Your grief may be simplified because you realize once and for all that you are not alone. It may get complicated because you begin to wonder if your grieving is worse than or better than the grief of others in the group. You confront your emotions differently when you're alone than you do when you're in a room filled with other people.

A group offers you the benefit of being in a room with others who may feel *just like you*. Think of it as having your own personal advisory committee on hand for all big decisions. Together you can share information on school memorials, family arguments and how to resolve them, and when it's "normal" to stop grieving. You'll find a list of support group resources at the back of the book.

You can also inquire about grief counseling groups in your community. Check the yellow pages under Counseling Services or Bereavement or start a group at your school. Your guidance counselor there can be helpful in getting one started. Don't underestimate all the resources at your disposal whether at home, at school, or in your neighborhood. Sometimes there are helpful groups you may not have considered right away, like kids from church or Hebrew school, summer campers, or even other kids on your hockey team.

There are so many people and places you can turn to when searching for the right support group.

- Mental health or other human service organizations

- Church, synagogue, or other spiritual homes

- School or university

- Hospice or bereavement services

- Funeral homes

- Physician (psychiatrist or even your family doctor)

- Someone else who has lost somcone

What Do I Do Now?

Once you have chosen a therapist or a counseling group and are proceeding with grief therapy, take another deep breath.

You have come a long way through grief. Congratulations on taking the steps it took to get here.

Therapy is almost never simple. It's not like you decide to go into it, and suddenly that black cloud you felt following you instantly vanishes. Counseling, like everything else, is work. What matters now is how you approach that work.

The relationship between you and your therapist promises to be one of the most unique you can ever experience. This person is meant to be there for you, and only you. Imagine that! No one to interrupt you, boss you around, or *not* listen. All this counselor wants and needs to do during your time together is listen to you and no one else.

Whatever you tell your therapist is sacred. In almost all cases, a therapist is not allowed to tell anyone what you say without your consent. The exception to this rule would occur if for some reason the therapist was fearful about your state of mind or thought you needed more serious evaluation or treatment. They would only reveal information as a way of further protecting you, in other words. It is always all about *you*.

As you enter into a "helping" relationship, make sure the process is completely collaborative. You're in charge of your own grief. He or she is there to help, not make you feel worse.

Important Words About Suicide

Sometimes because of special life circumstances, our grieving may be marked by confusion because we seem not to be feeling how we think we should. Perhaps the exercises in this book have brought no relief. Sometimes our feelings of loss may seem so tragic and pervasive that we believe we can no longer go on. Such feelings of despair and hopelessness may even lead us to think about suicide.

Your suicidal thinking may come from a wish to end the pain inside your mind and body. Right now, death may seem to you like the only way out. But it isn't.

Whether you are thinking about suicide because you feel hopeless or because the deceased committed suicide, it is *essential* that you talk to someone about it. This is something you need to address *immediately* with whatever therapist or counselor you visit. Do not be afraid if you feel helpless and suicidal. There is someone who can help you.

Suicidal feelings are a reality for many teens at many different times. During grief, these feelings should *never* be ignored or hidden away. Take them out and talk about them. You may need a counselor, medication, or a restful night's sleep — and a new perspective.

Unfortunately, the subject of suicide is so complex that it cannot be fully addressed in this grief book. There are, however, places to go and people to talk to. Look for them. You can *always* dial a suicide hotline, twenty-four hours a day.

Check the back of this book for other resources.

To everything there is a season,
A time for every purpose under heaven. . . .
A time to weep and a time to laugh,
A time to mourn, and a time to dance.

— Ecclesiastes 3:1,4

Conclusion

Life can only be understood backwards, but it must be lived forwards.

—Søren Kierkegaard

Getting through grief is a heroic journey. Surviving the death of someone you love is probably one of the most intense experiences you have ever had to face. As you look back through your Grief Journal and ahead into the unknown, how are you supposed to feel? Has someone's death presented a new way for you to see and experience your life? As you move forward, what are your expectations?

Grief can change everything. Has it?

Perhaps this book has challenged some of your perceptions about death, life, and everything else in between. Maybe it also offered comfort when you were feeling shocked, depressed, sad, or any other emotion. Hopefully, you have gained some kind of insight into yourself as you moved through grief.

Have you learned about the most heroic and deepest-feeling parts of yourself?

At the heart of every important story in mythol-

195

ogy, an individual is forced to confront death before he becomes a hero. The heroes of Greek myths faced death as menacing shadows or three-headed monsters, and yet they survived and came out through the other side, braver and wiser than before.

Author Joseph Campbell described a hero's mythic challenge as a "supreme ordeal," when a person stares into the eyes of death. Surviving this, that person is then transformed, or symbolically reborn.

Believe it or not, that person is *you*, right now.

You have made it through your own "supreme ordeal." That is grief. You are the hero in this story.

What is special about using Campbell's language to describe your experience is how well it represents a range of heroic journeys. Not only does it aptly explain how you made it through this grief, it also shows how you can survive *all* journeys in your life.

Grief may have taken you to a deep, dark, or sad place. But now it may heal you and raise you above all that has happened. Having taken a hero's journey, you are likewise joined with other mythic heroes of the past, present, and future. You need *never* be alone in any of it.

Examine where this journey has taken you so far; and then dream of where you may go next.

Keep remembering — but keep moving forward, too.

APPENDIX
Other Bereavement Resources

Continue to educate yourself about grief. Visit a library or bookstore, carefully select some books about bereavement, and read all you can about the grieving process. This will help you know what to expect and enable you to be more patient with yourself. Also, check out local or national grief organizations. The World Wide Web is a vast and helpful resource during any and all stages of grief.

Keep your eyes, ears, and heart open as you grieve. Other people's stories and experiences may help you to move on.

Reading Lists

Share good books on death, dying, and grief with your family or with friends. Remember that sometimes even a simple picture book might touch a deep feeling inside of you. The simpler the message, the more impact it may have.

Picture Books

A Little Bit of Robby by Barbara J. Turner
Badger's Parting Gifts by Susan Varley
Cat Heaven by Cynthia Rylant
The Dead Bird by Margaret Wise Brown
Dog Heaven by Cynthia Rylant
The Fall of Freddie the Leaf: A Story of Life for All Ages
    by Leo Buscaglia, Ph.D.
Hope for the Flowers by Trina Paulus
I'll Always Love You by Hans Wilhelm
The Jester Has Lost His Jingle by David Saltzman

Poppy's Chair by Karen Hesse
Rudi's Pond by Eve Bunting
Saying Goodbye to Daddy by Judith Vigna
The Tenth Good Thing about Barney by Judith Viorst
What's Heaven? by Maria Shriver
When Dinosaurs Die by Laurie Krasny Brown and Marc Brown

Novels and Plays

Adam's War by Sonia Levitin
Blackberries in the Dark by Mavis Jukes
Bridge to Terabithia by Katherine Paterson
Charlotte's Web by E. B. White
Chasing Redbird by Sharon Creech
Daddy's Climbing Tree by C. S. Adler
Death Be Not Proud by John Gunther
A Death in the Family by James Agee
Face at the Edge of the World by Eve Bunting
Fig Pudding by Ralph Fletcher
The Flip-Flop Girl by Katherine Patterson
Getting Near to Baby by Audrey Couloumbis
Hunter in the Dark by Monia Hughes and Clarke Irwin
I Never Promised You a Rose Garden by Joanne Greenberg
Jonathan Livingston Seagull by Richard Bach
Just One Tear by K. L. Mahon
The Last April Dancers by Jean Thesman
The Last Payback by James Van Oosting
A Lesson Before Dying by Ernest J. Gaines
Listen for the Fig Tree by Sharon Bell Mathis
Little Men by Louisa May Alcott
Little Women by Louisa May Alcott
Mick Harte Was Here by Barbara Park
Missing May by Cynthia Rylant
Nilda by Nicholasa Mohr
Nobody's Fault by Patricia Hermes

Ordinary People by Judith Guest
Our Town by Thornton Wilder
The Red Badge of Courage by Stephen Crane
A Ring of Endless Light by Madeline L'Engle
Sadako by Eleanor Coerr
The Secret Garden by Frances Hodgson Burnett
A Separate Peace by John Knowles
A Sound of Chariots by Mollie Hunter
Striking Out by Will Weaver
A Summer to Die by Lois Lowry
Swallowing Stones by Joyce McDonald
The Sweet Hereafter by Russell Banks
Tiger Eyes by Judy Blume
Where the Lilies Bloom by Vera and Bill Cleaver
Whirligig by Paul Fleishman
Winter Holding Spring by Crescent Dragonwagon
You Shouldn't Have to Say Good-bye by Patricia Hermes

Nonfiction

The Courage to Grieve by Judy Tatelbaum
Death is Hard to Live With by Janet Bode
The Grieving Teen by Helen Fitzgerald
Living When a Loved One Has Died by Earl Grollman
Part of Me Died, Too by Virginia Lynn Fry
Straight Talk About Death for Teenagers by Earl Grollman
Tuesdays with Morrie by Mitch Albom
*When a Friend Dies: A Book for Teens About Grieving and
    Healing* by Marilyn E. Gootman, Ed.D.
When Bad Things Happen to Good People by Rabbi Harold S.
    Kushner

Music

You may have songs that tug at your heartstrings. Play them. Here are some suggestions for artists whose tunes might feel comforting as you grieve. Don't forget, however, that your choice of music doesn't need to be mellow. Put on house music and dance your grief away, turn up the classical radio station and take a nap, or blast some rap or heavy metal and feel angry. It's up to you.

The Beatles
Sarah McLachlan
Pete Seeger
Judy Collins
Natalie Merchant
Carole King
Melissa Etheridge
Alanis Morrisette
Cat Stevens
Aimee Mann
Van Morrison
James Taylor

One joy scatters a hundred griefs.

— Chinese proverb

Movies

When someone has died, you may want to view home movies of that person. You may also want to rent a movie about loss or grief to let off steam or have a good cry. The following movies may be a good place to start. Of course, the subjects of some films may be upsetting, so consider watching them with a friend, older sibling, or parent, rather than watching them by yourself. And don't forget that watching a happy movie like a comedy or fantasy may be more uplifting to watch at this time of grief. Ask friends and family for other recommendations.

Always
A River Runs Through It
All Dogs Go to Heaven
All Quiet on the Western Front
Bambi
The Big Chill
Corrina, Corrina
E.T.: The Extra-Terrestrial
Field of Dreams
Forrest Gump
Fried Green Tomatoes
It's a Wonderful Life
Little Women
Longtime Companion
Marvin's Room

Men Don't Leave
My Life
My Life as a Dog
One True Thing
Ordinary People
Permanent Record
Philadelphia
Romeo + Juliet
Stand By Me
Terms of Endearment
Titanic
To Gillian on Her 37th Birthday
Truly, Madly, Deeply
The Sweet Hereafter

Organizations and Web Sites

1000 Deaths

A person who commits suicide dies once, but those left behind die a thousand deaths, trying to relive those terrible moments and understand why. SOLOS (Survivors of Loved Ones' Suicides) has organized this site as a forum for mourners.
http://www.1000deaths.com/

About.com Grief Collection

Poems and stories that tell of the mental suffering, distress, or coming to terms with the loss of a friend or family member. Written by and for teens.
http://teenwriting.about.com/teens/teenwriting/library/collections/blcoll120.htm

ADD

A collection of articles and suggestions on dealing with death and grief from People Against Drunk Driving.
http://www.add.ca/grieving.htm#gr07

Amanda the Panda

Amanda the Panda provides support to children and their families who are grieving the death of a family member through accident, illness, suicide, or homicide. The support is provided through weekend camps, support groups, home visits, fun days, school presentations, pen pal programs, Halloween and Christmas parties, birthday cards, and remembrances on the anniversary of the death.
1000 73rd Street, Suite 12
Des Moines, Iowa 50311
Phone (515) 223-4847
Fax (515) 223-4782
http://www.amandathepanda.org/

The American Foundation of Suicide Prevention

This organization offers a complete list of support groups throughout the country.
Phone (888) 333-2377

Bereaved Parents of the USA

A Journey Together, Betty R. Ewart, Editor
326 Longview Avenue
Lewisburg, West Virginia 24901
Phone/fax (304) 645-3048
http://www.bereavedparentsusa.org/

Bereavement Magazine

A Magazine of Hope and Healing Includes an on-line magazine and archive of subjects, cards, booklets, music, videos, "hope" gifts, e-sympathy messages, e-memorials, and more.
Bereavement Publishing, Inc.

5125 North Union Boulevard
Colorado Springs, Colorado
80918
(888) 60-4HOPE (4673)
http://www.bereavementmag.com/

The Compassionate Friends, Inc.

A national not-for-profit self-help
support organization that offers
friendship and understanding to
families who are grieving the
death of a child of any age, from
any cause. There is no religious
affiliation. There are no
membership fees or dues, and all
bereaved family members are
welcome.
P.O. Box 3696
Oak Brook, Illinois 60522-3696
Phone (630) 990-0010
Fax (630) 990-0246
http://www.compassionatefriends.
org

Crisis, Grief, and Healing

Webmaster: Tom Golden
A web site where men and women
can discuss, chat, or simply
browse to understand and honor
the many different paths to
healing strong emotions.
http://www.webhealing.com/
1grief.html

The Dougy Center

The National Center for Grieving
Children and Families provides
support and training locally,
nationally, and internationally to
individuals and organizations

seeking to assist children and
teens in grief.
P.O. Box 86852
Portland, Oregon 97286
http://www.dougy.org

Fernside, A Center for Grieving Children

An organization that reaches out
to the community with support
and advocacy for grieving
children and their families.
2303 Indian Mound Avenue
Cincinnati, Ohio 45212
Phone (513) 841-1012
http://www.fernside.org

GriefNet

An Internet community of persons
dealing with grief, death, and
major loss. One of the oldest grief
sites on the Net; founded by
Cendra Lynn. Offers many grief-
related e-mail discussion lists for
specialized types of bereavement.
e-mail editor@griefnet.org
http://www.rivendell.org

Julie's Place

Julie's Place is designed for kids
and teens to interact with other
kids and teens who have lost a
sibling.
http://www.juliesplace.com

KidSaid

A safe place for kids to share and
to help one another deal with
grief about any of their losses. It's
a place to share and deal with

feelings, to show artwork and stories, to talk about pets, to meet with one's peers.
http://www.griefnet.org/KIDSAID

Motherless Daughters, Inc.
Provides support, community, and resources to women and girls who have experienced early mother loss. Brings together motherless daughters to encourage healing and to promote awareness about the long-lasting effects of such a loss.
P.O. Box 663, Prince Street Station
New York, New York 10012
Phone (212) 614-8041
Fax (212) 614-8047

Mothers Against Drunk Driving (MADD)
Mothers Against Drunk Driving is a not-for-profit grassroots organization with more than six hundred chapters nationwide. MADD is not a crusade against alcohol consumption. Its focus is to look for effective solutions to drunk driving and underage drinking problems, while supporting those who have already experienced the pain of these senseless crimes.
Phone (800) GET-MADD
http://www.madd.org/victims/default.shtml

Motivating Moments
An on-line collection of motivational quotes and inspirational stories, including pages on getting through grief.
http://www.motivateus.com

NAMES Project
The NAMES Project Foundation sponsors and displays the AIDS Memorial Quilt to help bring an end to the AIDS epidemic. The goals of the NAMES Project are to provide a creative means for remembrance and healing, illustrate the enormity of the AIDS epidemic, increase public awareness of AIDS, assist with HIV prevention education, and raise funds for community-based AIDS service organizations.
310 Townsend Street, Suite 310
San Francisco, California 94107
Phone (415) 882-5500
Fax (415) 882-6200
e-mail Info@AIDSQuilt.org
http://www.AIDSQuilt.org

Old Bones
An unusual and thought-provoking destination for the mourner, this site showcases photos and messages from headstones from a hundred to three hundred years ago.
http://www.oldbones.net/index.htm

Rainbow Bridge
On-line pages devoted to pet loss. Remembering all kinds of loved pets in memorial pages, articles, poems, and other tributes.

e-mail meggie@rainbow-bridge.org
http://rainbowbridge.tierranet.com/bridge.htm

Rainbows
An international organization providing a bridge to emotional healing for children, adolescents, and adults confronting death, divorce, or other painful family transition "because it doesn't need to hurt forever."
2100 Golf Road #370
Rolling Meadows, Illinois 60008-4231
Phone (800) 266-3206
http://www.rainbows.org

SA\VE
Suicide Awareness\Voices of Education
To educate about suicide prevention and speak for suicide survivors.
7317 Cahill Road,
Suite 207
Minneapolis, Minnesota 55424-0507
Phone (952) 946-7998
e-mail save@winternet.com
http://www.save.org

TAG: Teen Age Grief, Inc.
Not-for-profit organization that provides grief support training for dealing with bereaved teens.
P.O. Box 220034
Newhall, California 91322-0034
Phone (661) 253-1932

Fax (661) 245-2536
www.smartlink.net/~tag/

The Virtual Memorial Garden
A place to celebrate family, friends, and pets and to tell others about them and why they were special. You can make a web page memorial here.
http://catless.ncl.ac.uk/vmg/

Virtual Pet Cemetery
You can create a message and memorial at this site for a pet that has died.
www.mycemetery.com

Bibliography

21st Century Dictionary of Quotations, edited by the Princeton Language Institute. Princeton: The Philip Leif Group, Inc., 1993.

The Book of Positive Quotations, compiled and arranged by John Cook. Minneapolis: Fairview Press, 1997.

The Courage to Grieve: Creating Living, Recovery and Growth Through Grief. Judy Tatelbaum. New York: Harper & Row Publishers, 1980.

Death is Hard to Live With: Teenagers Talk About How They Cope with Loss. Janet Bode. New York: Bantam Doubleday Dell Books for Young Readers, 1993.

Folklore on the American Land. Duncan Emrich. Boston: Little, Brown and Company, 1972.

Grief: Climb Toward Understanding. Phyllis Davies. San Luis Obispo, California: Sunnybank Publishers, 1987.

The Grief Recovery Handbook, Revised Edition. John W. James and Russell Friedman. New York: HarperPerennial, 1998.

Growing Through Grief: A K-12 Curriculum to Help Young People Through All Kinds of Loss. Donna O'Toole. North Carolina: Compassion Books, 1996.

Healing After Loss: Daily Meditations for Working Through Grief. Martha Whitmore Hickman. New York: Avon Books, Inc., 1994.

Hope for the Flowers. Trina Paulus. New Jersey: Paulist Press Inc., 1972.

In the Midst of Winter: Selections from the Literature of Mourning, edited by Mary Jane Moffat. New York: Vintage Books, 1982.

Light from Many Lamps: A Treasury of Inspiration, edited and with commentary by Lillian Eichler Watson. New York: Simon & Schuster, 1988.

The Mourning Handbook. Helen Fitzgerald. New York: Simon & Schuster, 1994.

On Death and Dying. Elisabeth Kubler-Ross, M.D. New York: Scribner, 1997.

Part of Me Died, Too: Stories of Creative Survival Among Bereaved Children and Teenagers. Virginia Lynn Fry. New York: Dutton Children's Books, 1995.

Seasons of Prosperity: An Intentional Prayer Book. Toni Stone. Williston, Vermont: Toni Stone, 1996.

A Time to Grieve: Meditations for Healing After the Death of a Loved One. Carol Staudacher. San Francisco: HarperCollins, 1994.

A Time Remembered: A Journal for Survivors. Earl A. Grollman. Boston: Beacon Press, 1987.

what have you lost? poems selected by Naomi Shihab Nye, photographs by Michael Nye. New York: Greenwillow Books, 1999.

When a Friend Dies: A Book for Teens About Grieving and Healing. Marilyn E. Gootman, Ed.D. Minneapolis: Free Spirit Publishing, 1994.

When Bad Things Happen to Good People. Rabbi Harold S. Kushner. New York: Avon Books, 1989.

The Writer's Journey. Christine Vogler. Studio City, California: Michael Weise Productions, 1992.

Author Biographies

Laura Dower has written and compiled numerous books for children and young adults, including the six-book nonfiction series *Real Teens: Diary of a Junior Year*, and an anthology about peace. She lives in New York.

Elena Lister, M.D. is a practicing psychoanalyst and adult, adolescent, and child psychiatrist. She has been counseling, teaching, and speaking about grief with parents, children, and professionals for nearly a decade. Dr. Lister currently serves as Clinical Assistant Professor of Psychiatry at Cornell University Medical College in New York City and as Collaborating Psychoanalyst at the Columbia Psychoanalytic Center. She speaks and consults regularly at hospitals and private schools in the New York area, especially on subjects of grief and loss. Dr. Lister lives in New York with her husband, daughter, and son.

Permissions